A+CROSS AMERICA

By Mary C. Spence

A+CROSS AMERICA

While taking long car trips, we passed many Crosses along the way and I would wonder who lost their life, how many people were affected and what was their story?

Here are a few stories I can share.

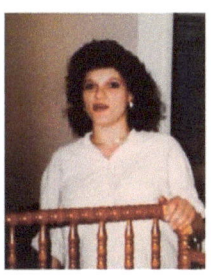

Years ago, my sister lost a good friend, Candy, in a car accident while in Seattle. She went on a trip and never returned. She was so young, as well as her husband and baby. I heard that he found out the exact location where she died and put a cross to mark the spot of her death. That was the first time I had ever heard of such a thing but thought it was a great tribute. That was over 40 years ago!

On my first job, returning back to work after a long holiday weekend, I was told my boss died in a tragic accident while driving his sports car on a curvy road. Never to be seen again. Does he have a cross, I wonder?

I lost my grandfather unexpectedly in a car accident on 79th and Harlem, Worth, IL due to a drunk driver. I hope to get the strength to put a cross there someday.

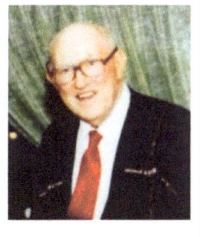

Losing someone this way is very tragic indeed. Putting up a Cross has become iconic.

I can only imagine the stories waiting to be told.

I'd like this book to be a memorial for those who lost their lives in such a tragic way and as a healing connection for those they left behind.

You can find more pictures of Crosses on my website: **www.acrossamerica-home.com.**

Mary C. Spence

A+CROSS AMERICA

By Mary C. Spence

On a recent road trip, my daughter and I took these photos. Unlike any long car game that quickly loses appeal, we were entranced with these crosses and what their stories might be.

I have photographed crosses along roadsides for years, and found each one to be different and hauntingly beautiful. While not meant to be intrusive, I feel these photographs offer a silent voice to the possible story behind them as a way of communication from here and beyond.

Mary C. Spence

Driving on a highway

Down a country road

Around the corner

Next to a stop sign

In the middle of a field

Near a busy gas station

Just beyond a hill

By the railroad tracks

In a park or in a field

Another Cross... Another story

One, two, three and four

Plain white or wood

Marked and unmarked

Names and dates, faded flowers,

Pictures....candles and lots

Tears I'm sure

Another Cross, Another story.

Somebody's lost loved one.

Whose we wonder?

Dread in the Details of time, day or nite

Stuck in the season of rain, or snow

Still we wonder? But No answers.

We may never know.

Young or old, but not forgotten

Another Cross, Another story.

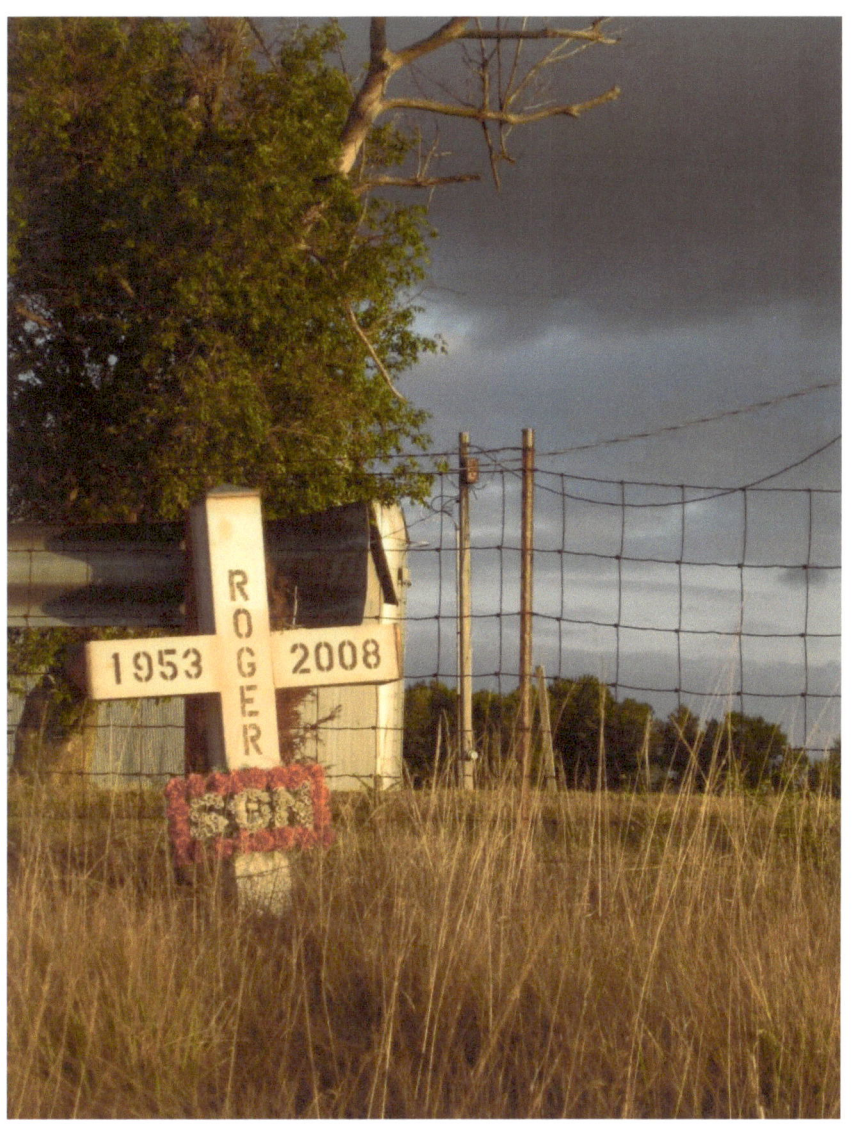

Driving on a highway

Down a country road

Another cross. Another story.

Somebody's lost loved one.

Whose, we wonder?

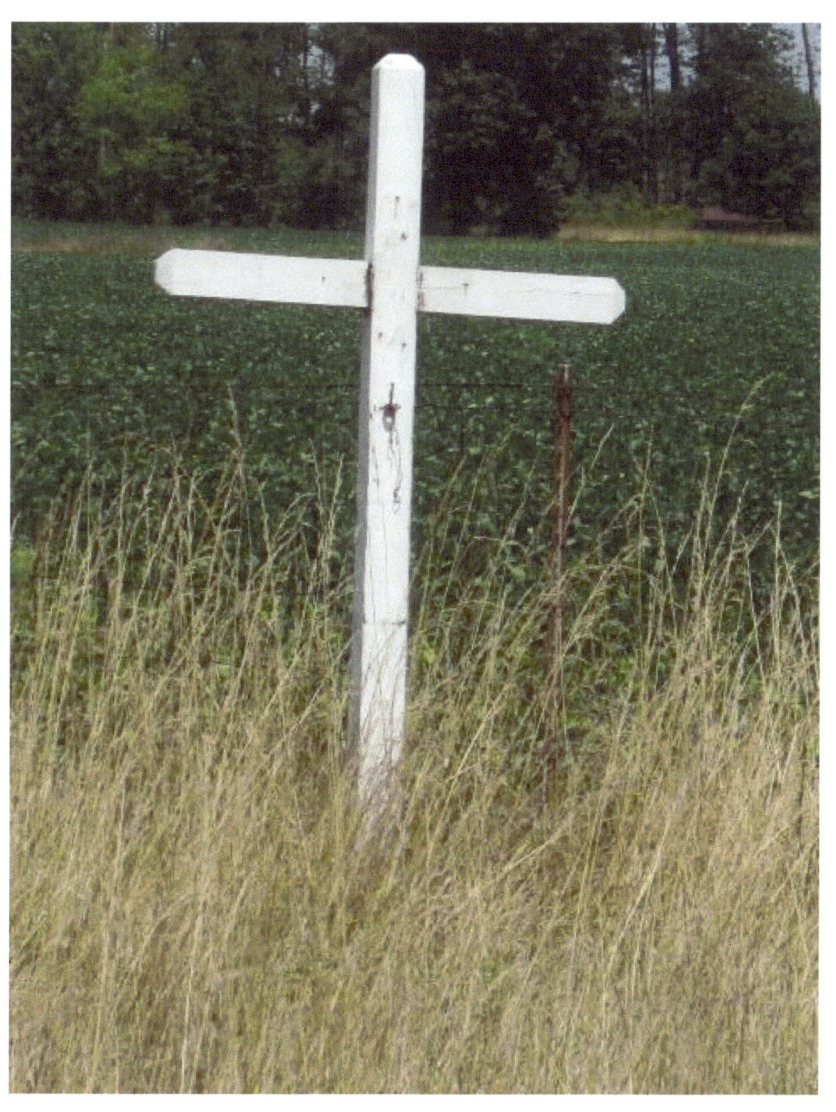

In the middle of a field

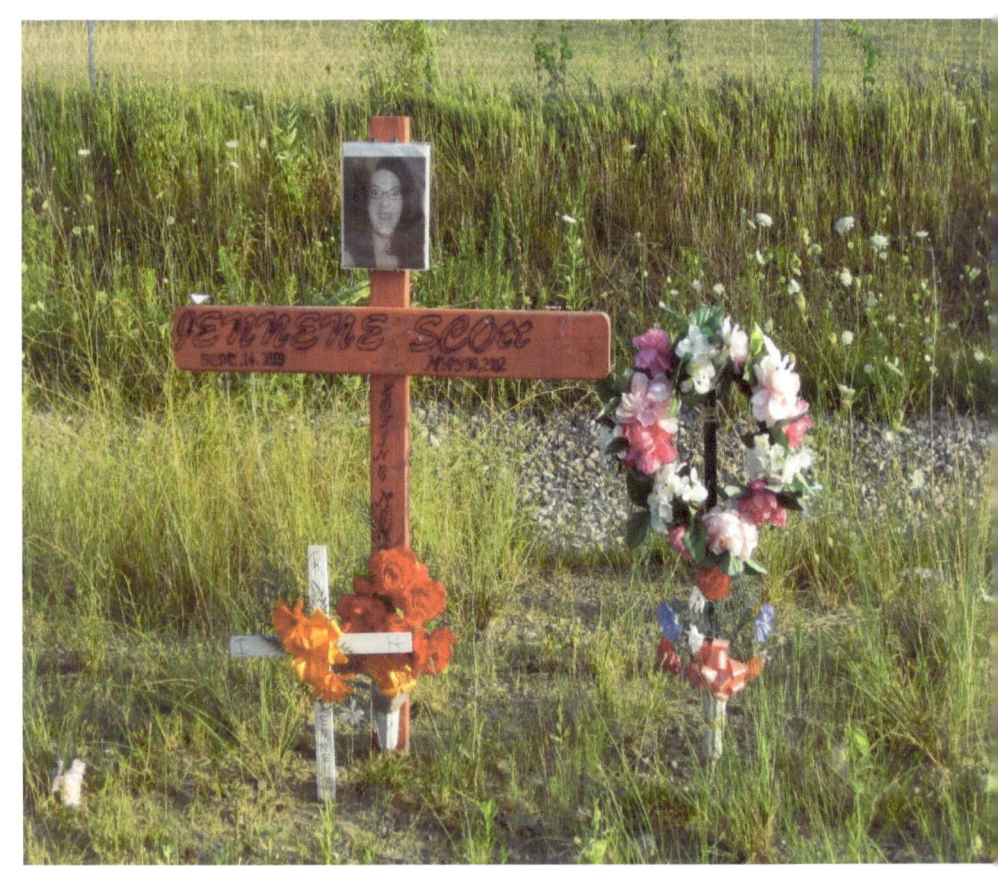

One, two, three

Plain, white, red,

names and dates, faded flowers,

Pictures....

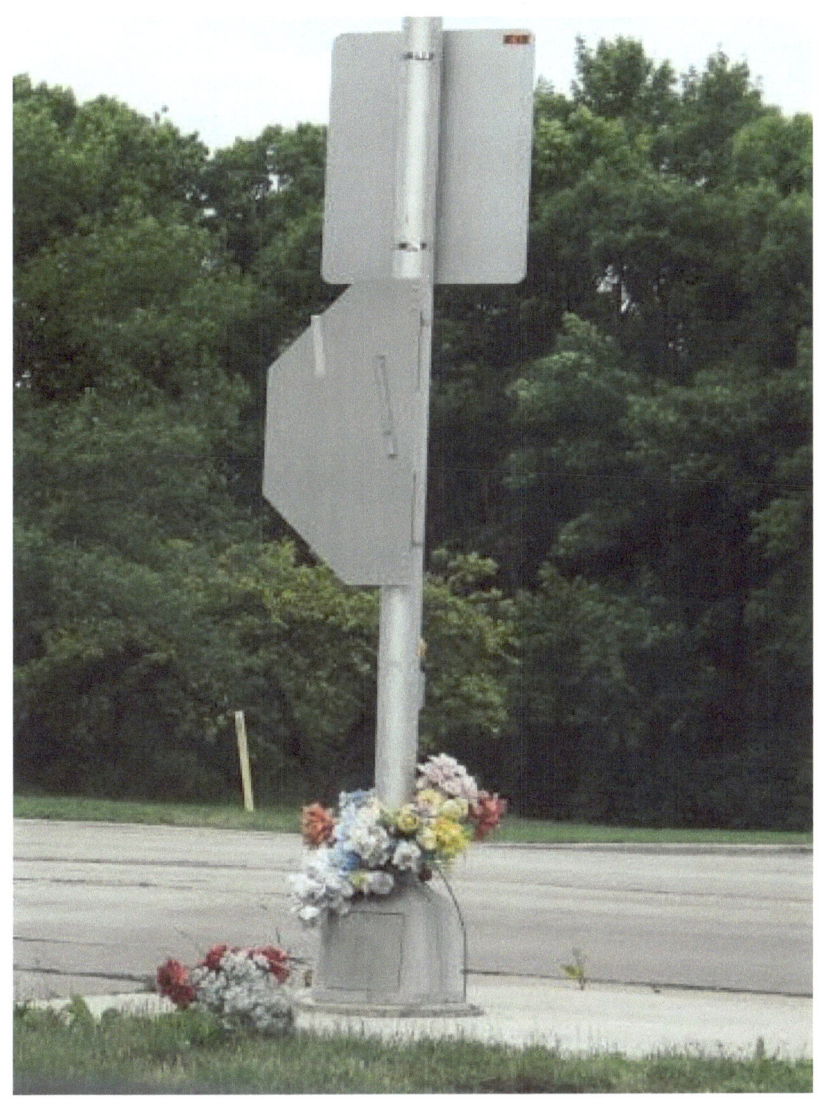

Around the corner
and
Next to a stop sign

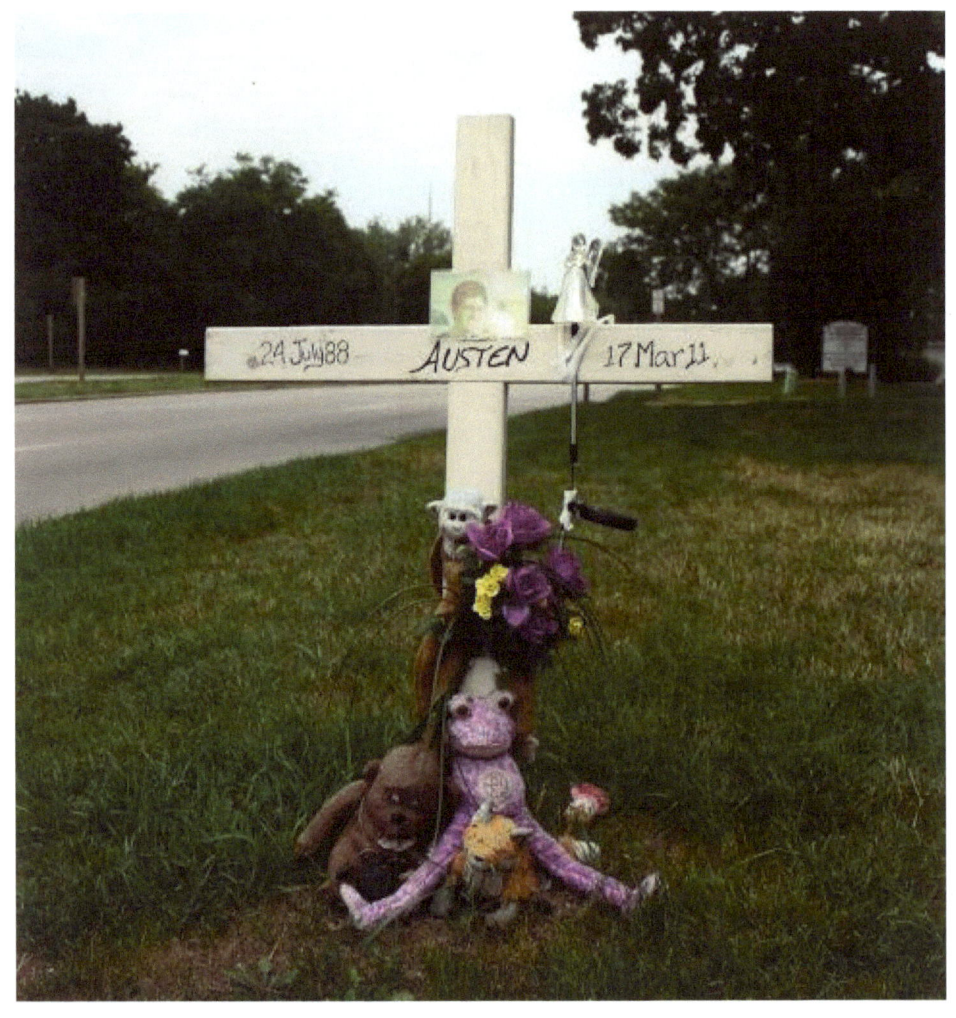

**Flowers to mark
and
stuffed animals to watch over
          broken hearts.**

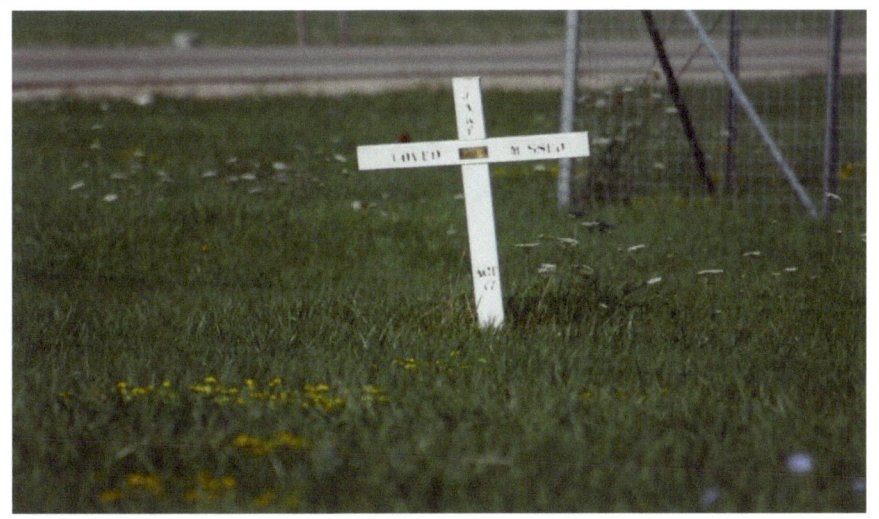

A Cross from different angles

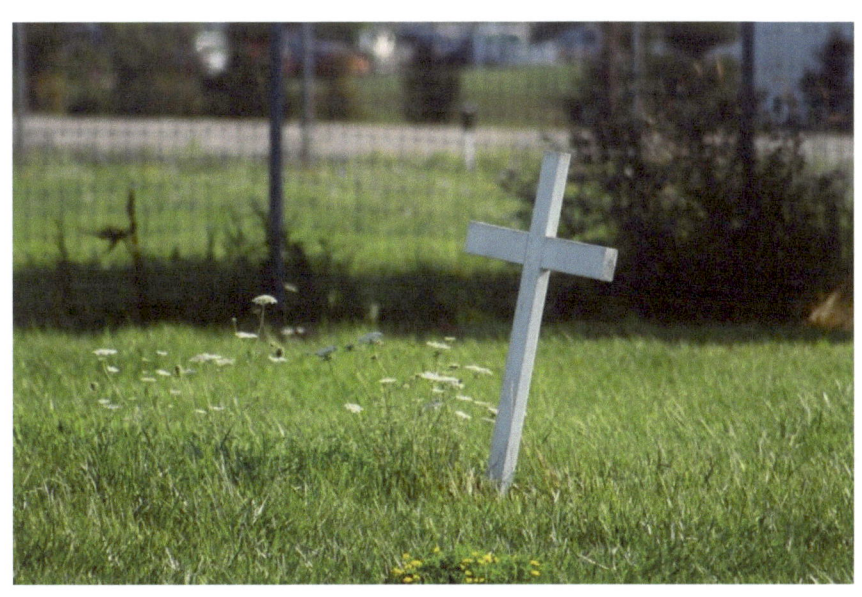

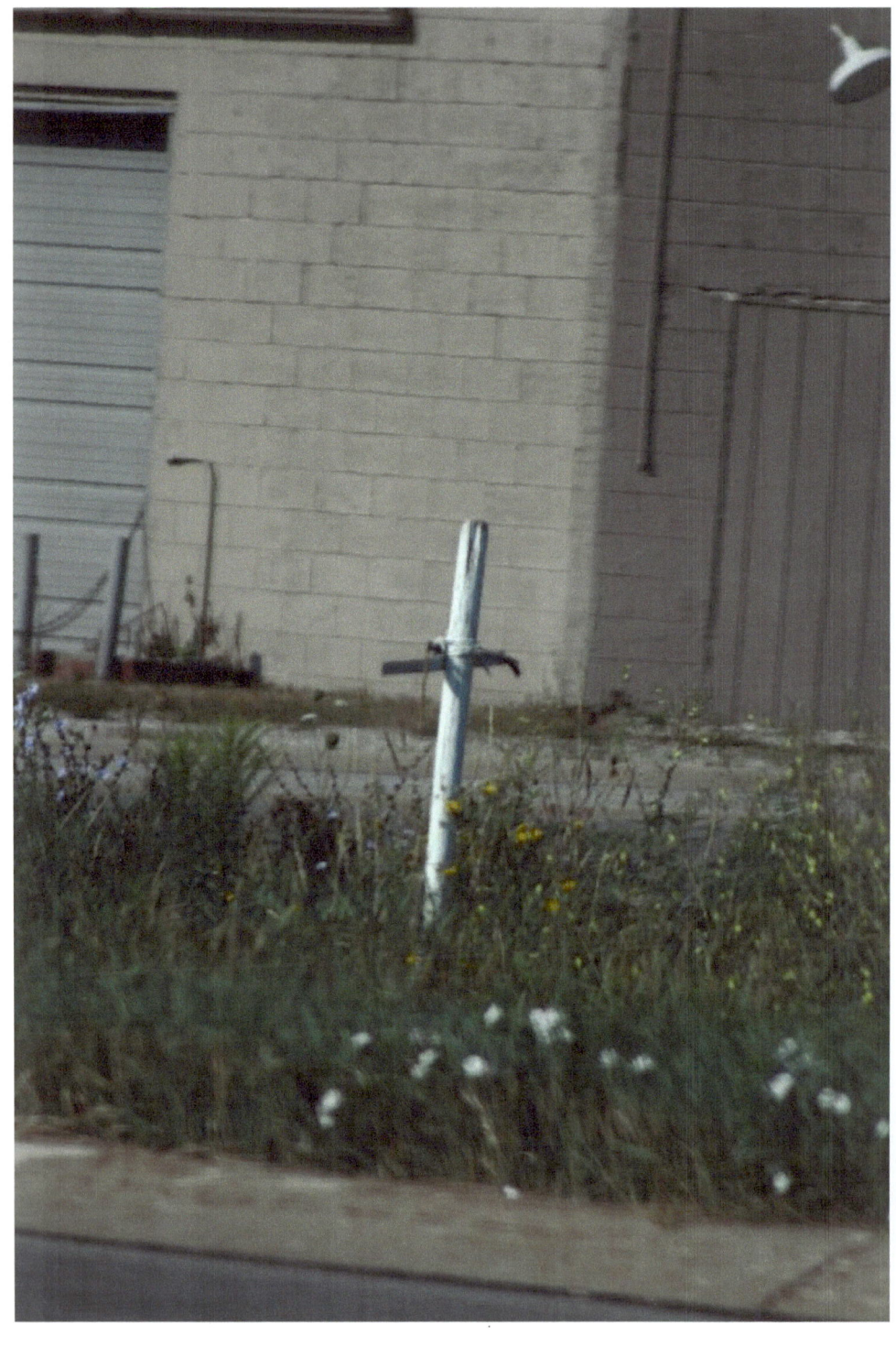

on the outskirts of town we pass this cross and it reminds us of how fragile life is.

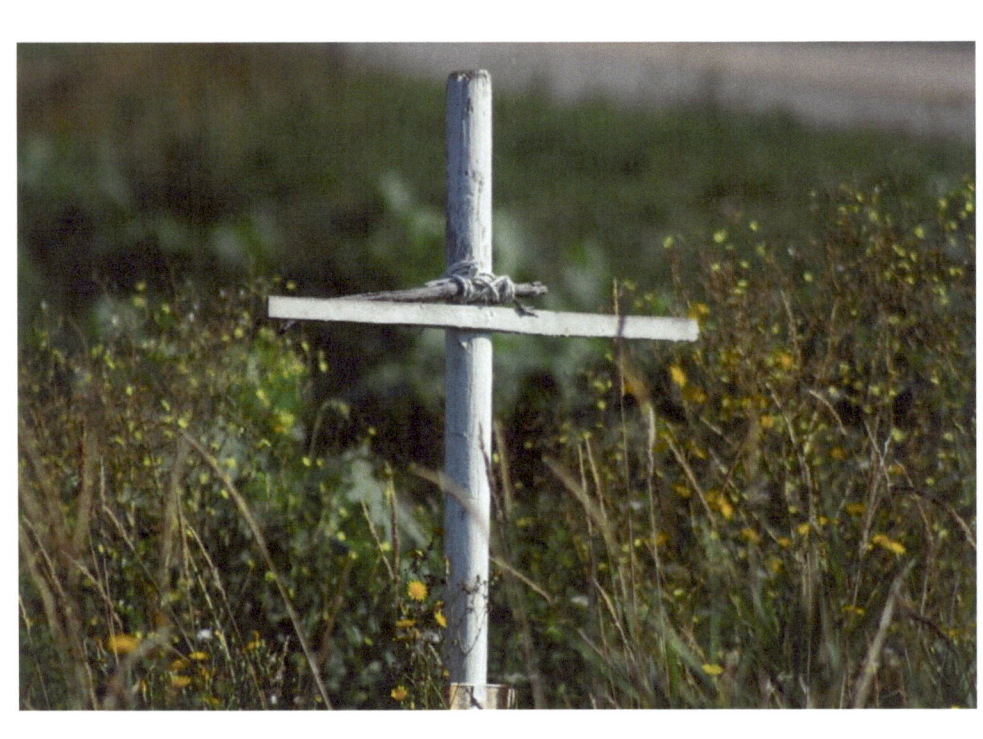

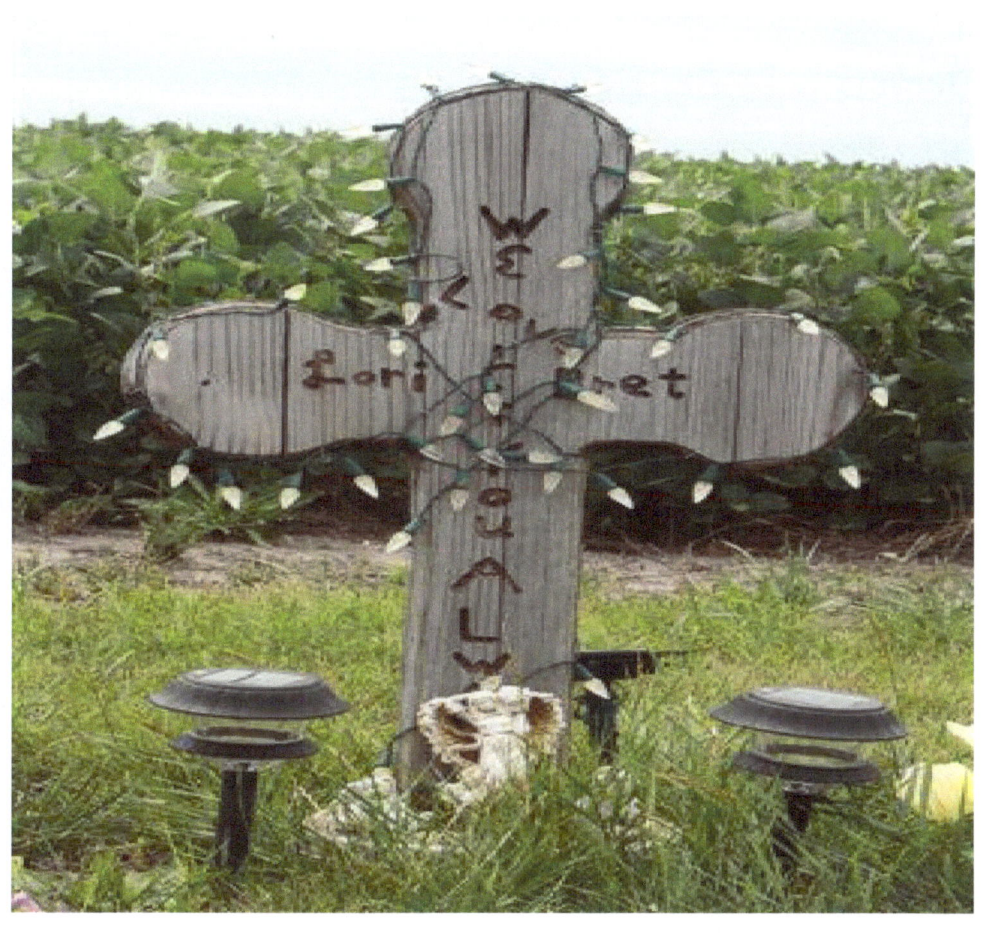

On a country road where beans grow on

near the high school they will never know.

Death has no boundaries,

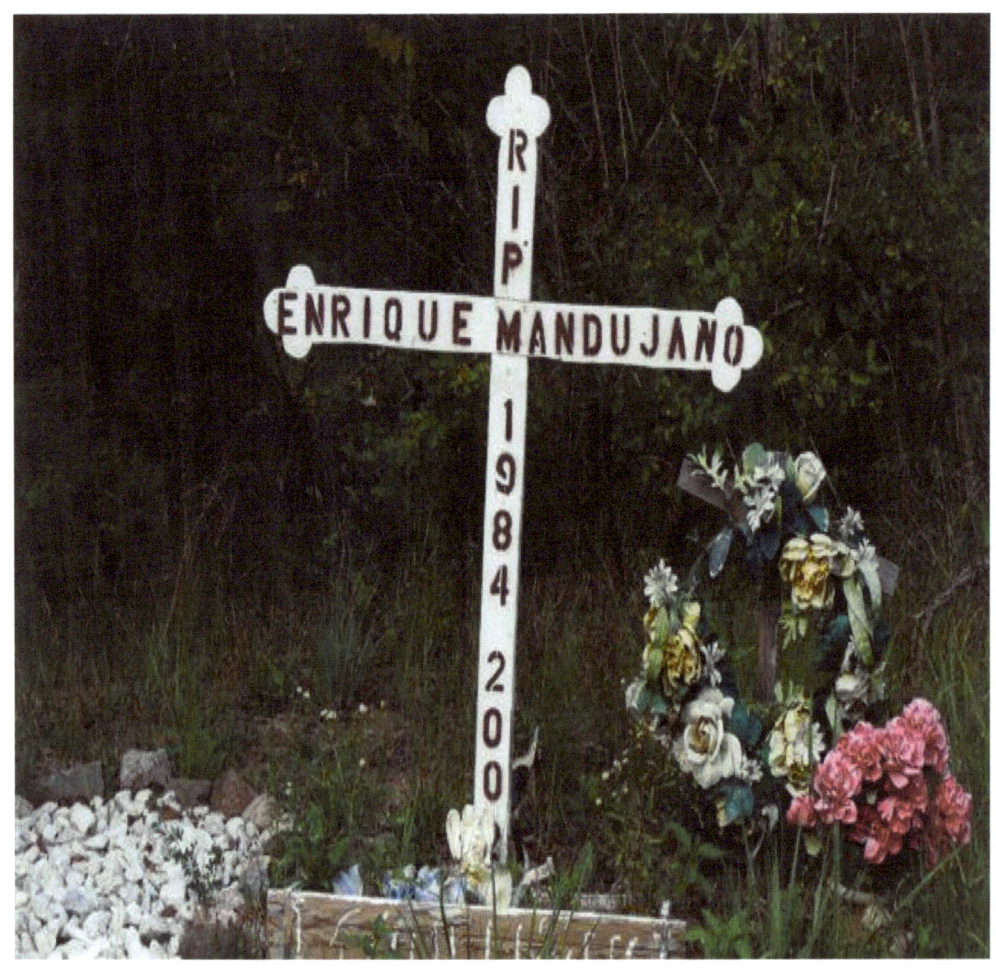

nor discriminates

Can there ever be Peace?

or Justice?

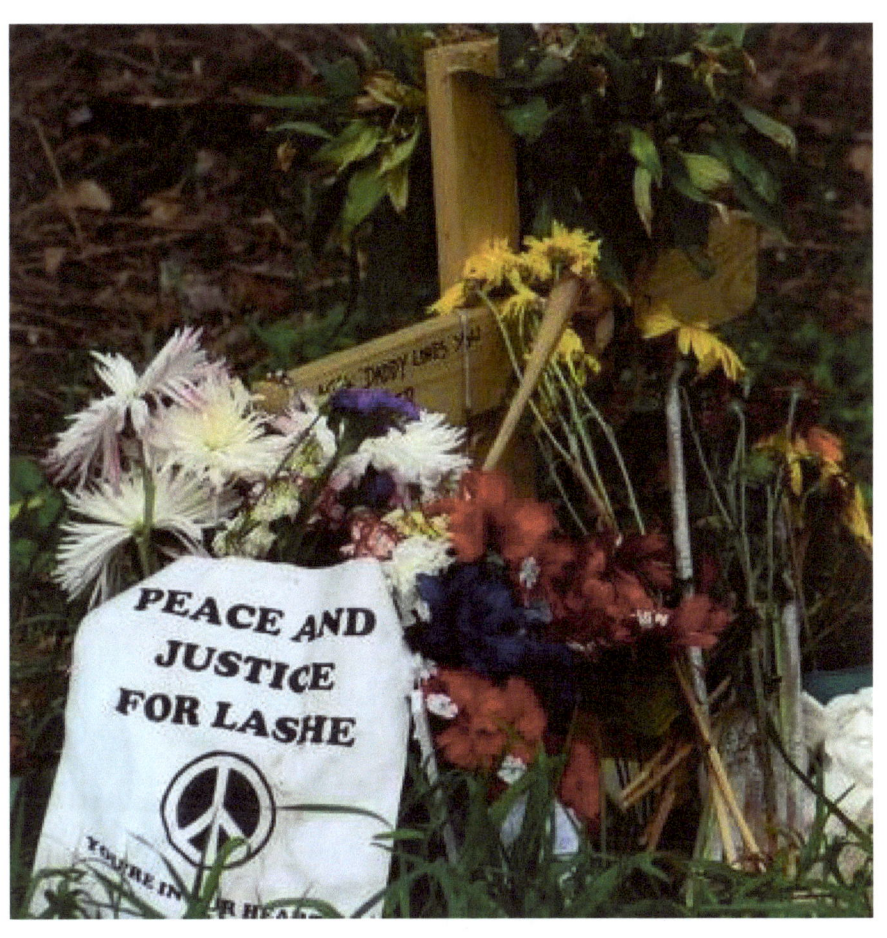

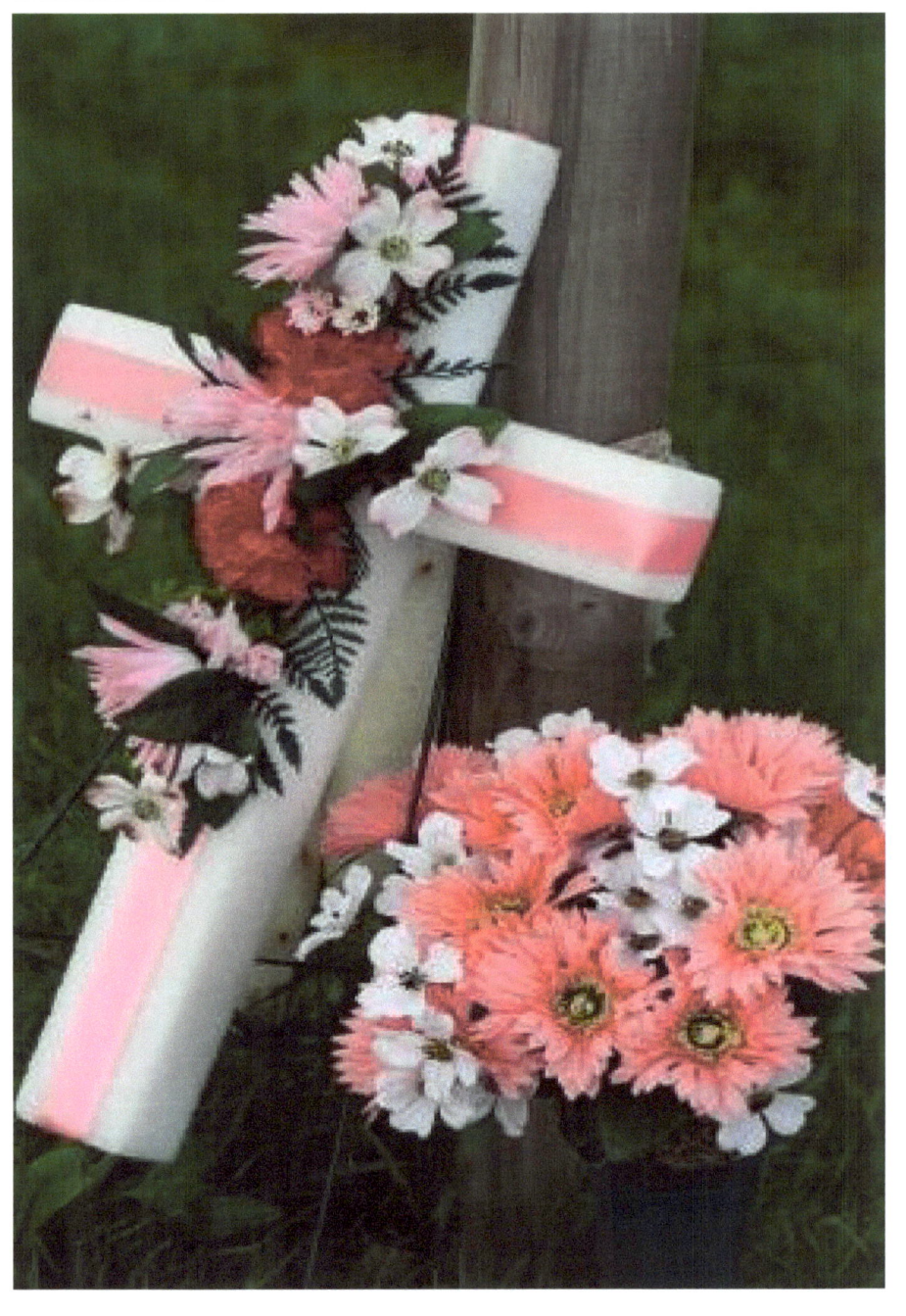

Or just beautiful symbols of love.

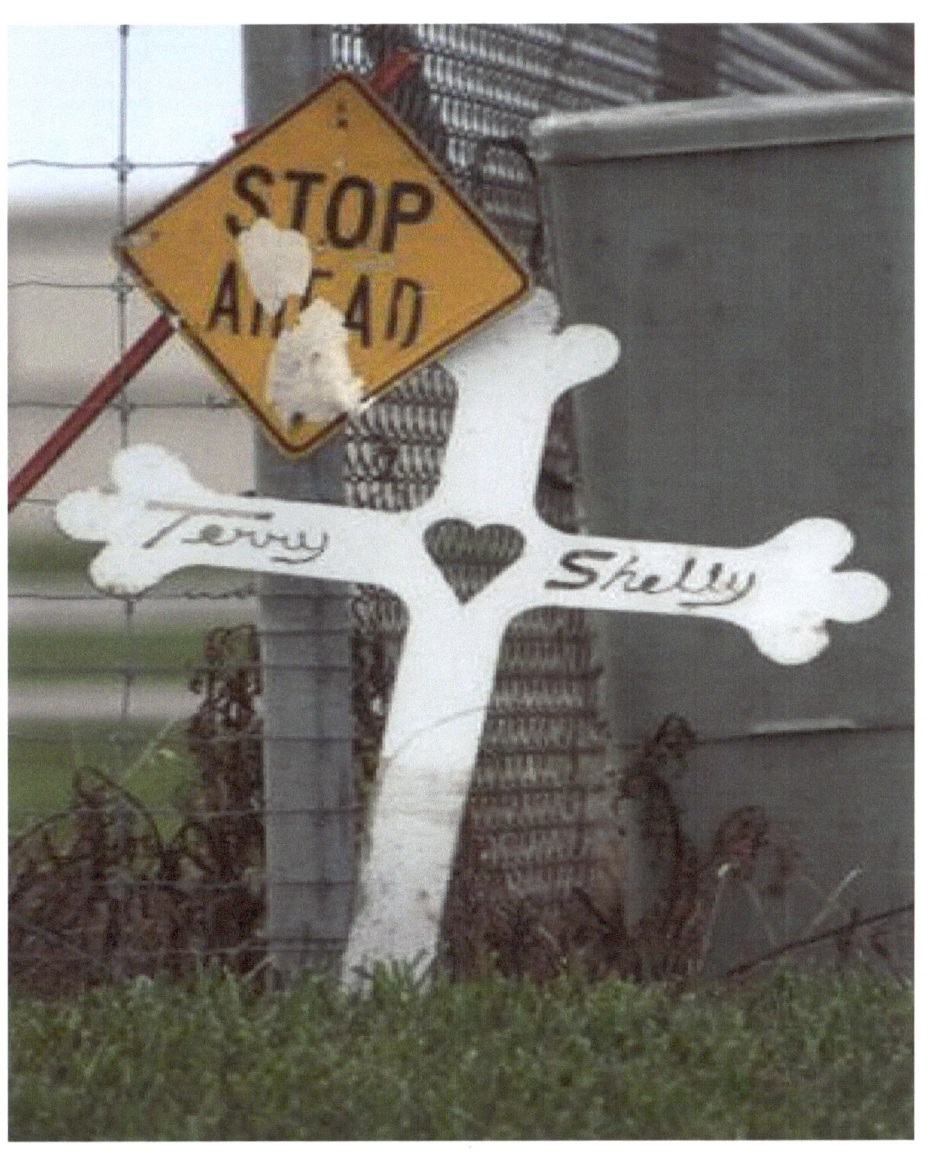

Death stops us all................................

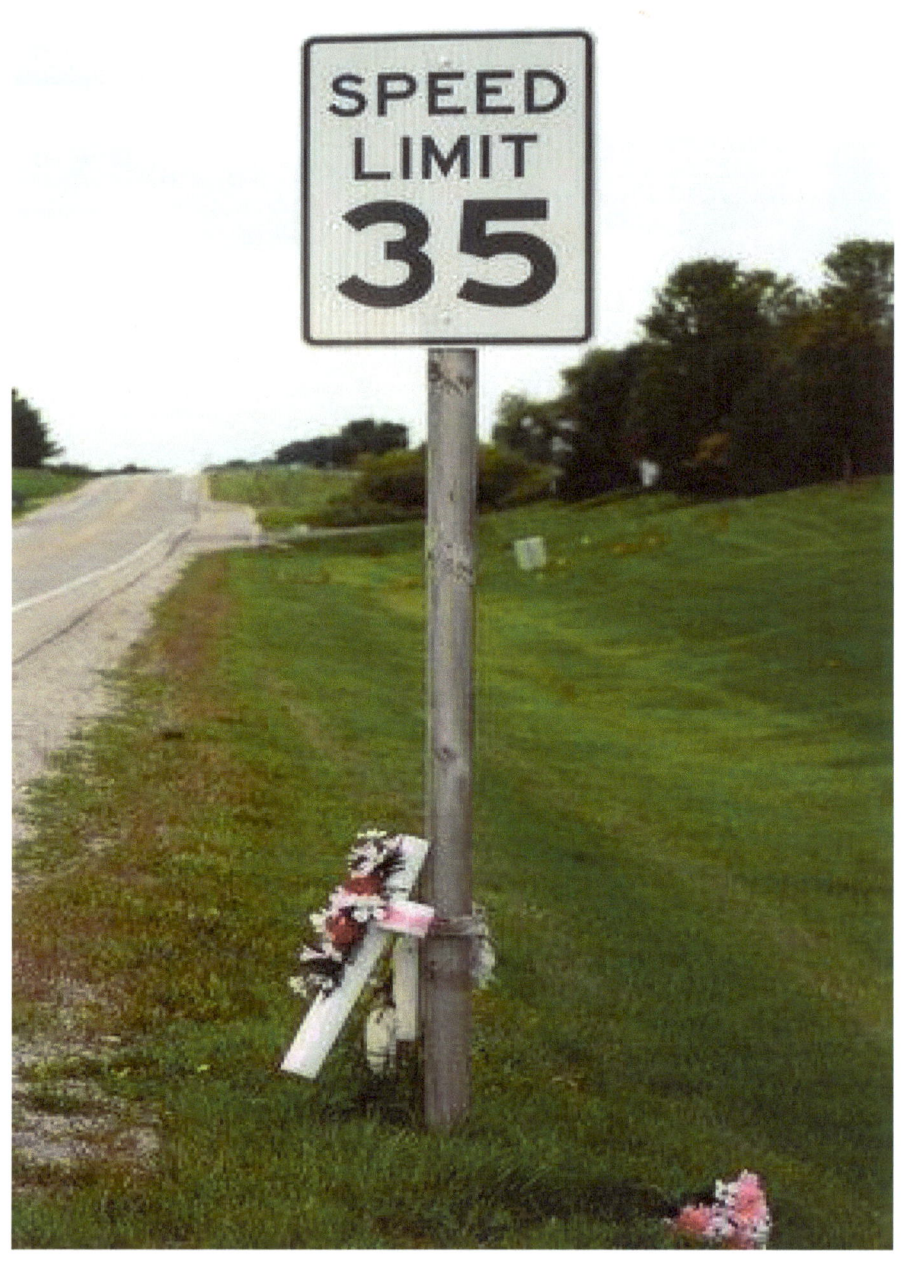

No matter how fast we are going.

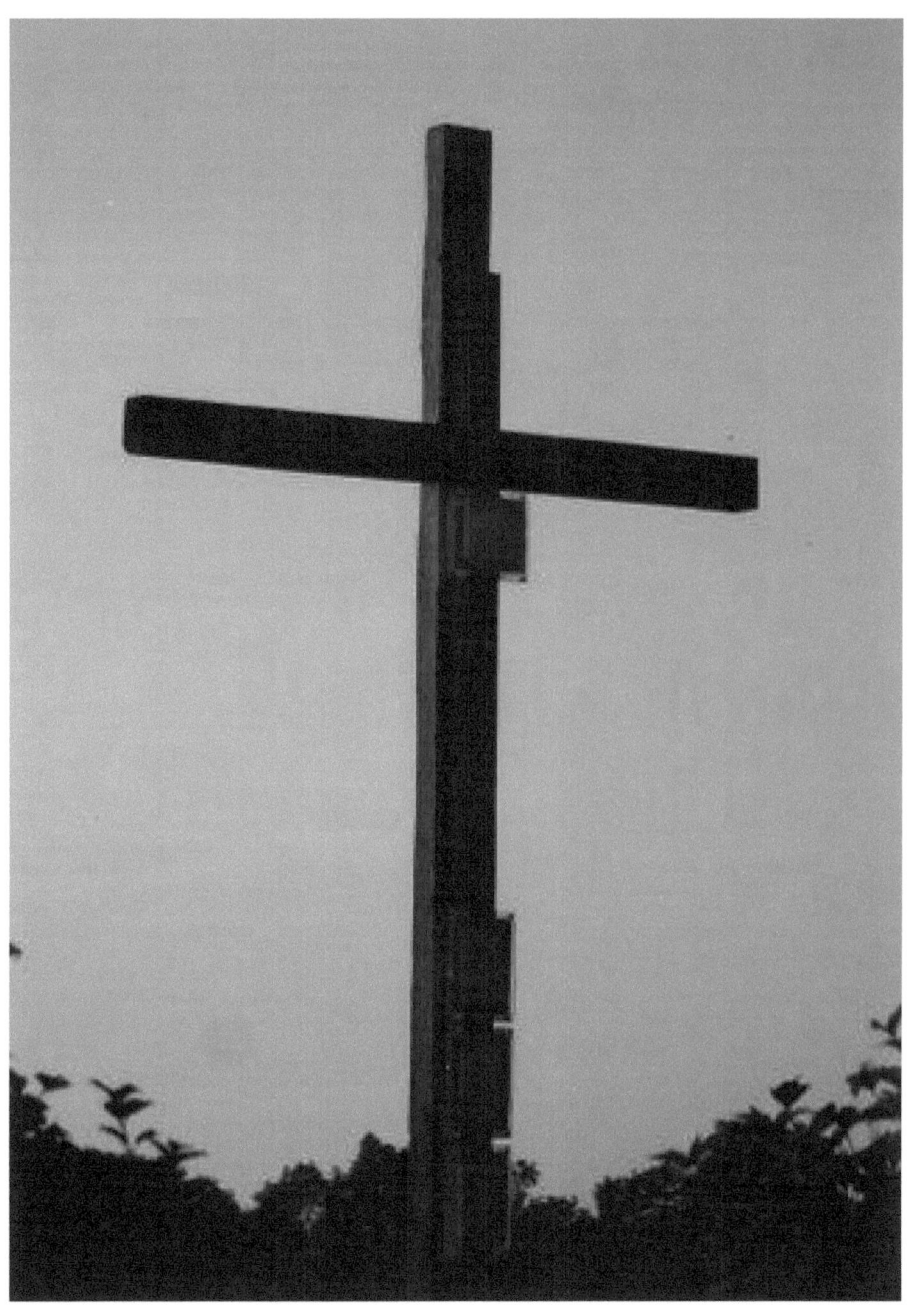

Morning

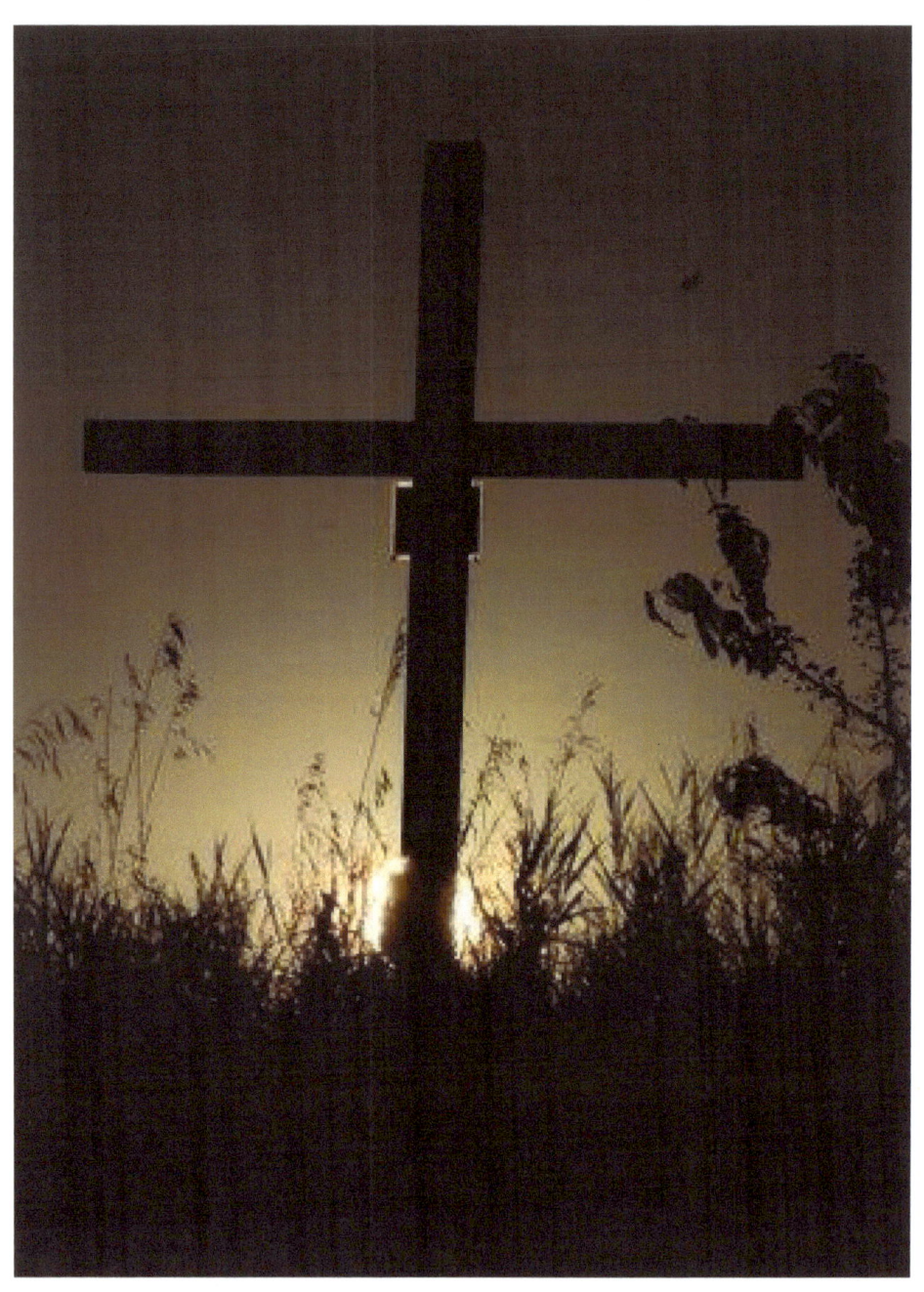

Night

It's everywhere ....

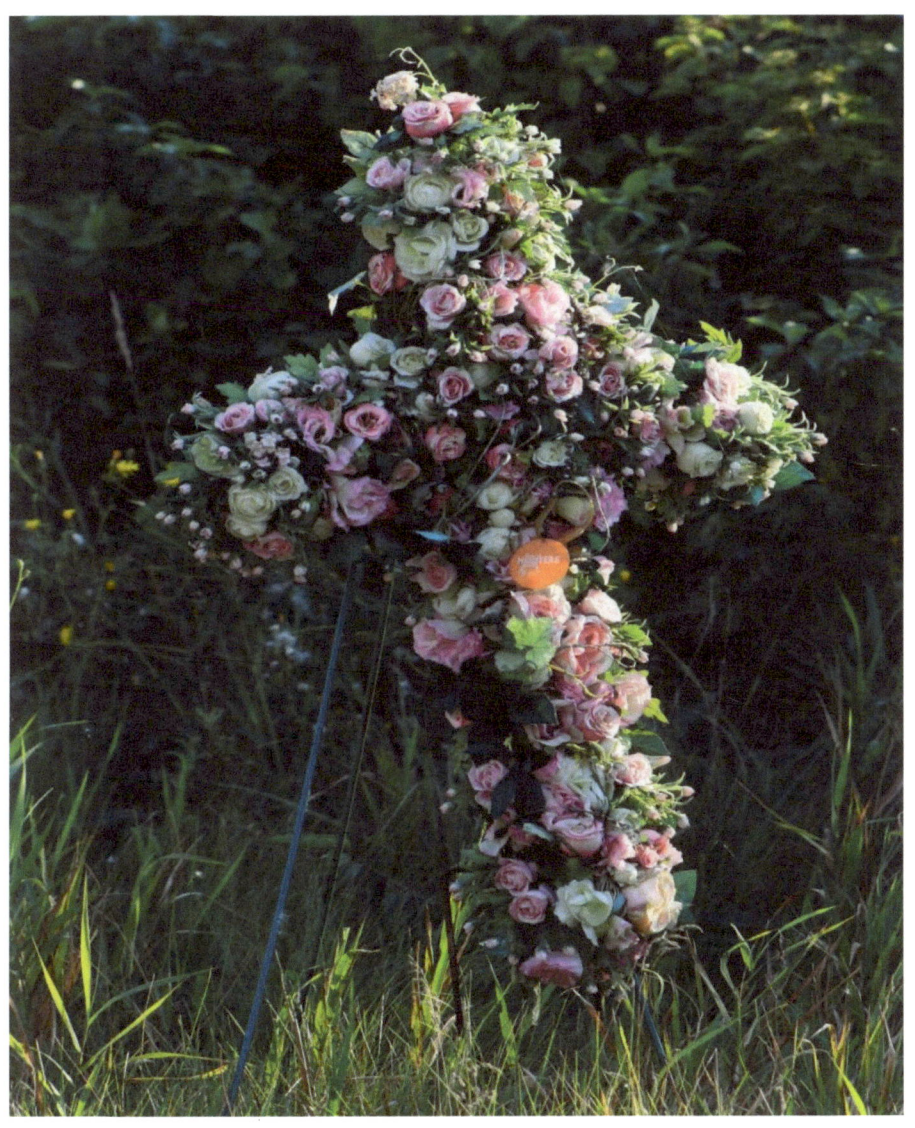

And touches all of us

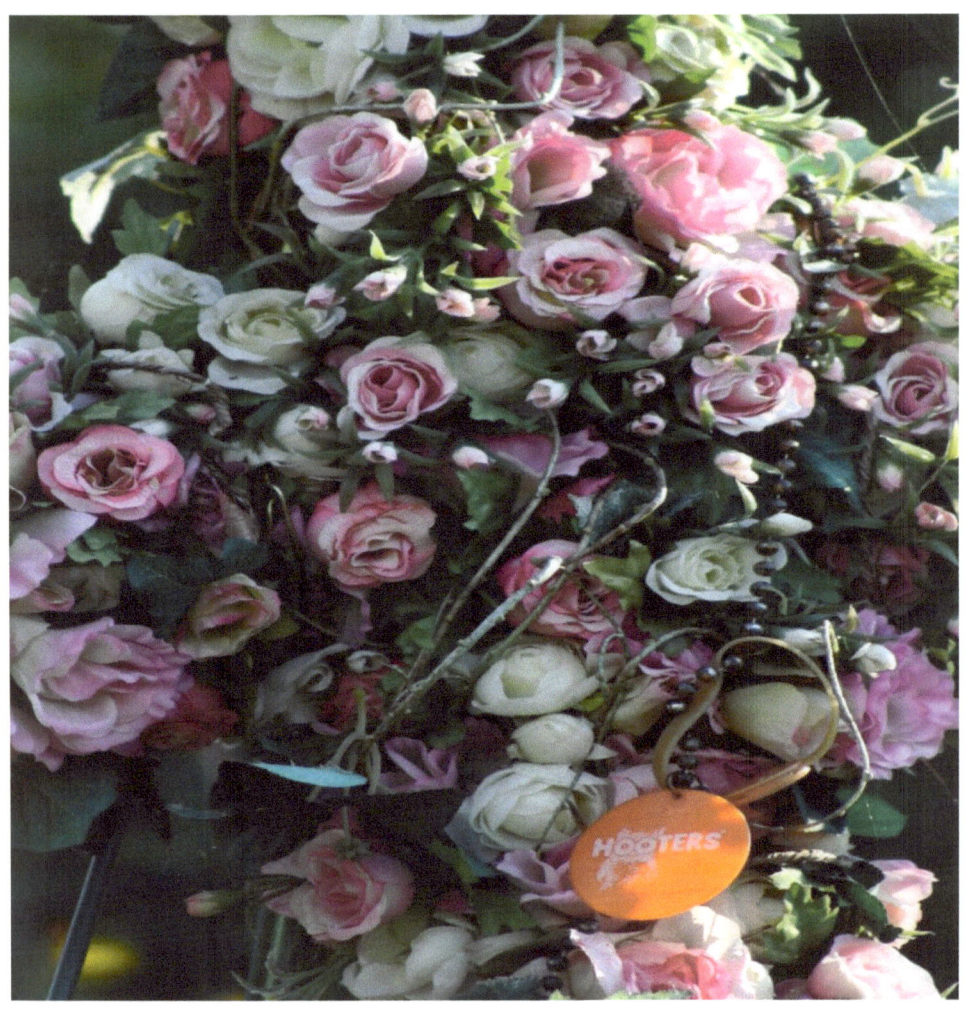

It's a shocking reminder that

when we are in pain

we are not alone.

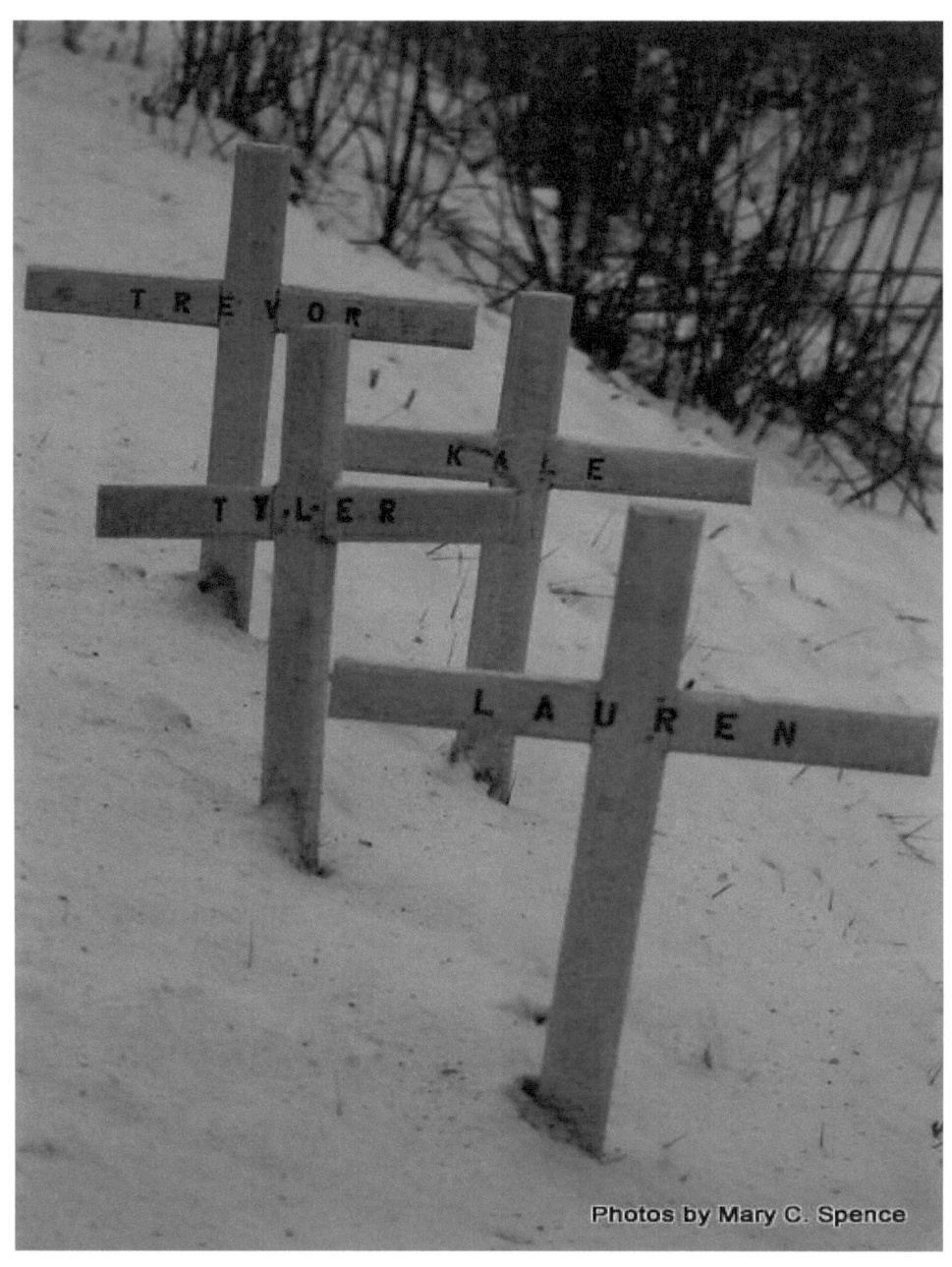

Photos by Mary C. Spence

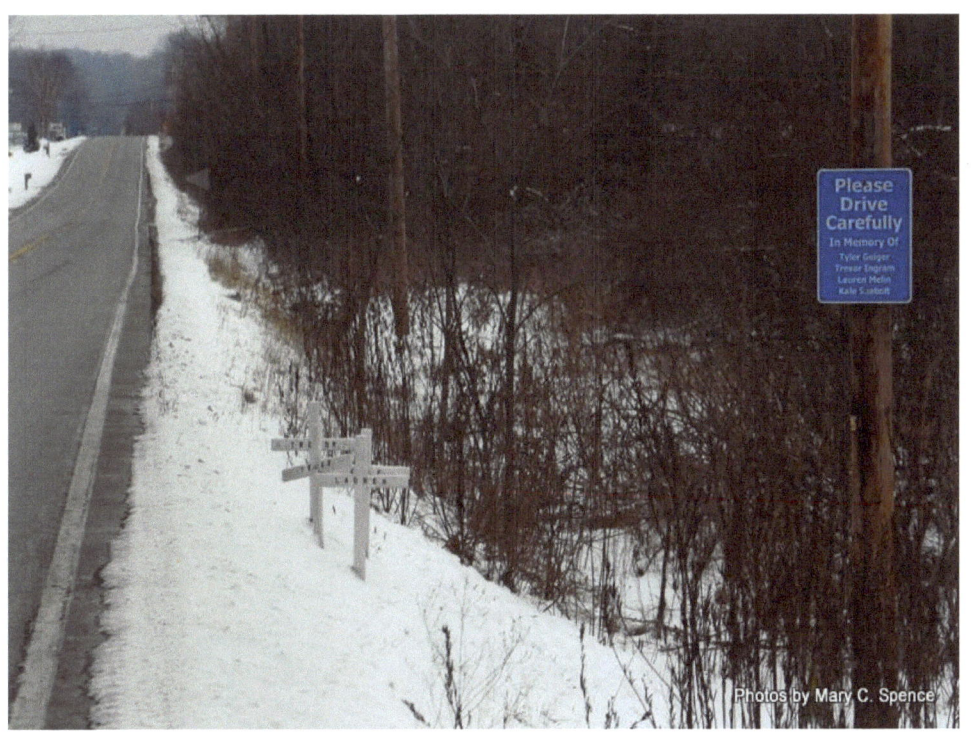

Nothing can prepare anyone....

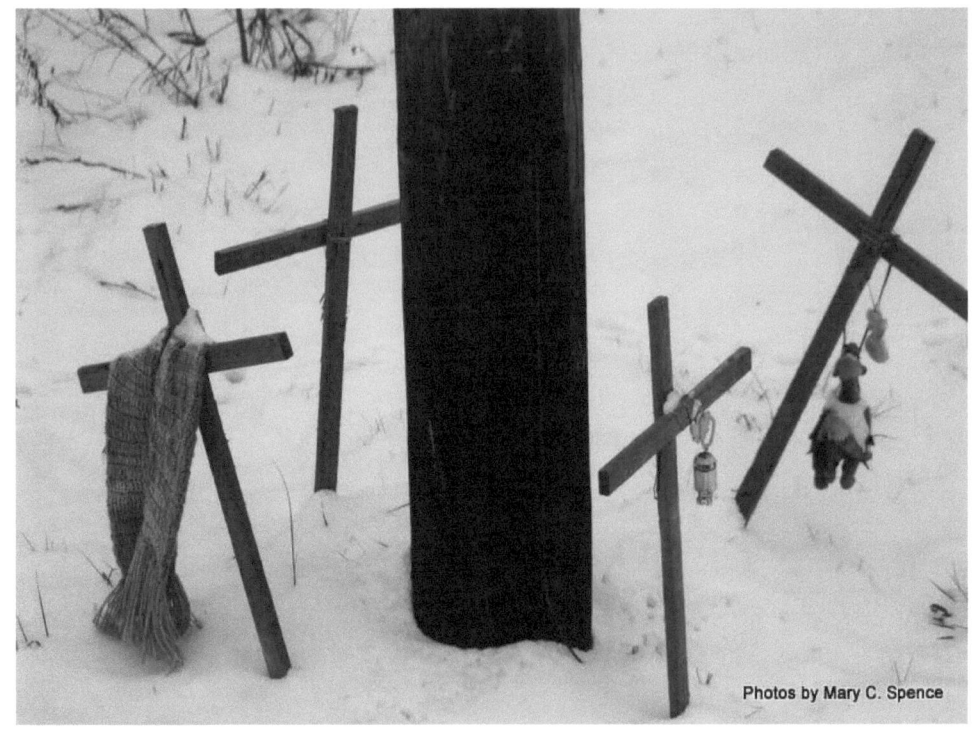

Photos by Mary C. Spence

For death...

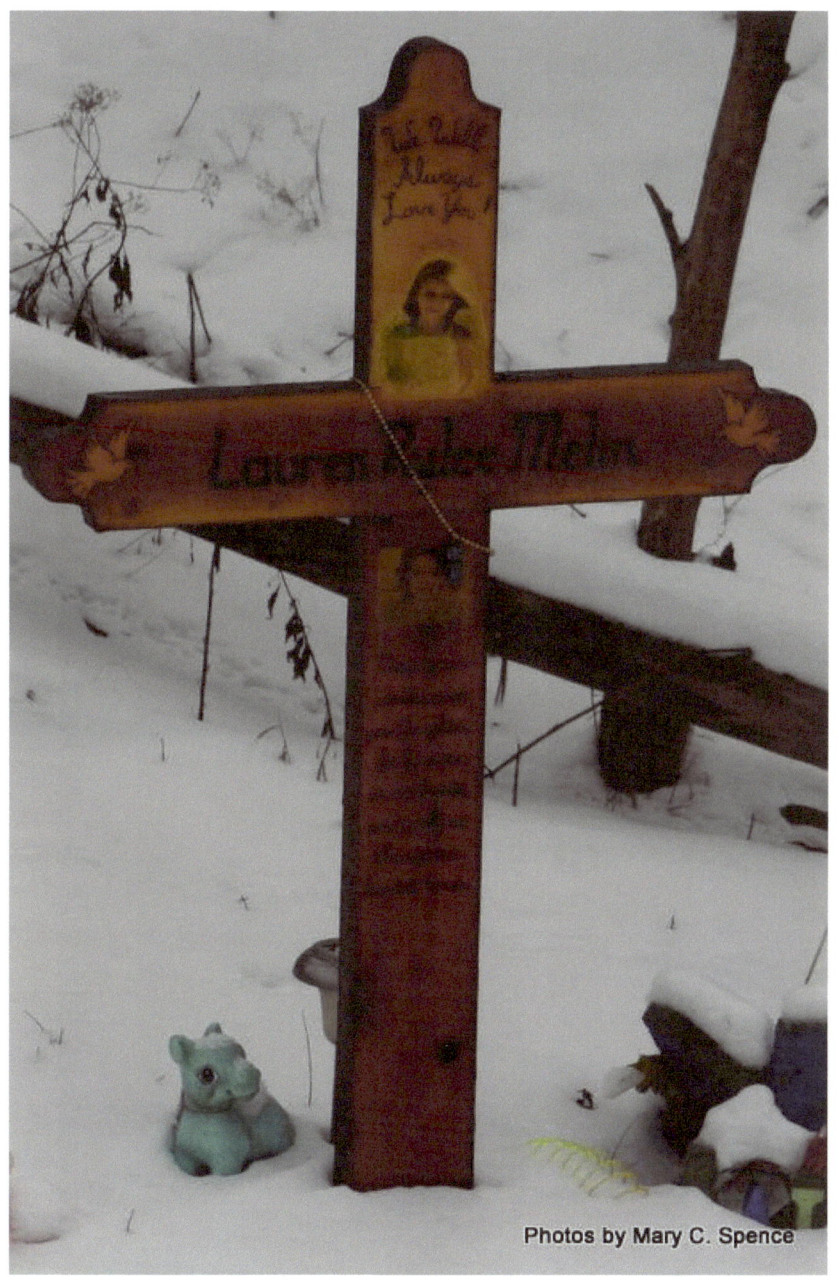

...or loss so young and dear...

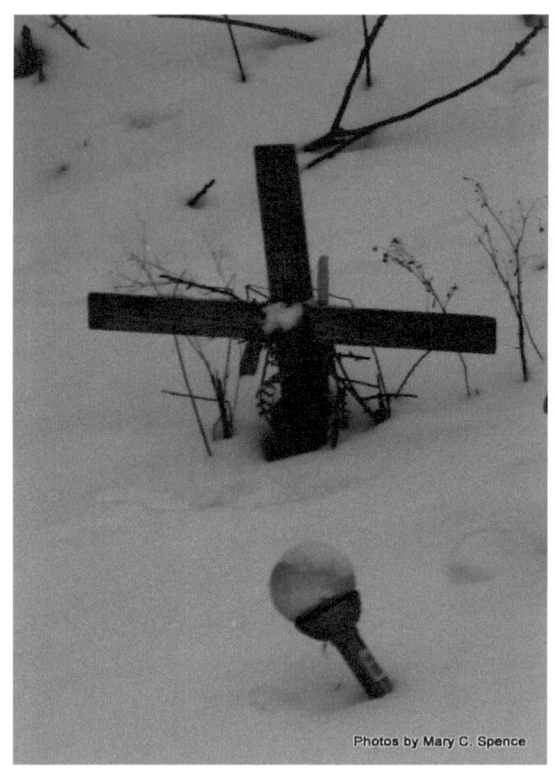

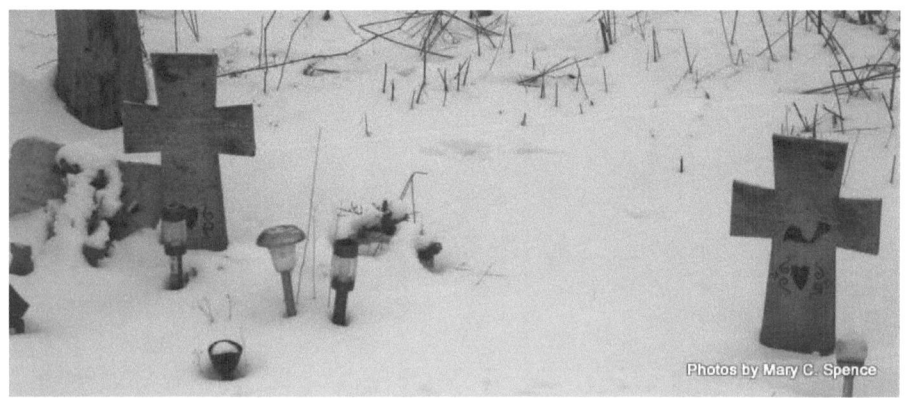

Photos by Mary C. Spence

or so many

Photos by Mary C. Spence

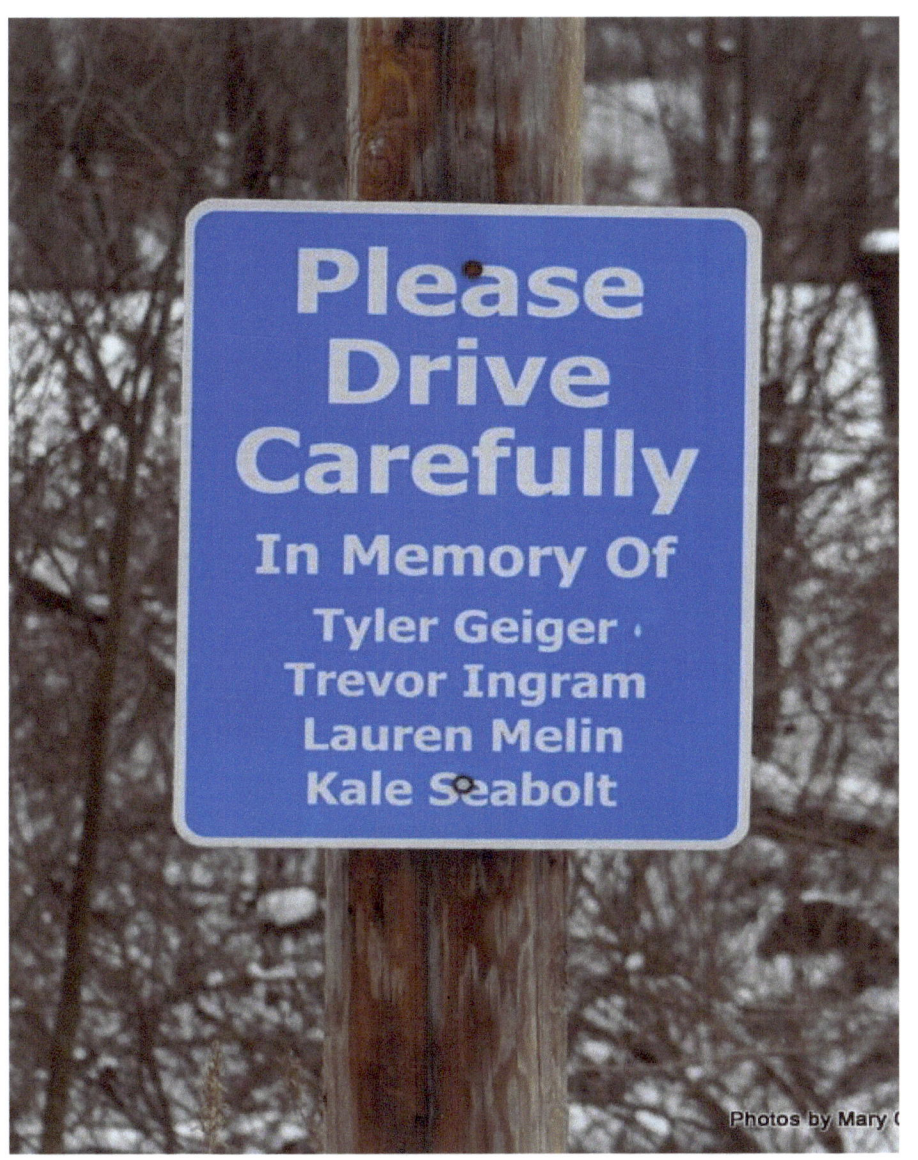

Please Drive Carefully
In Memory Of
Tyler Geiger ·
Trevor Ingram
Lauren Melin
Kale Seabolt

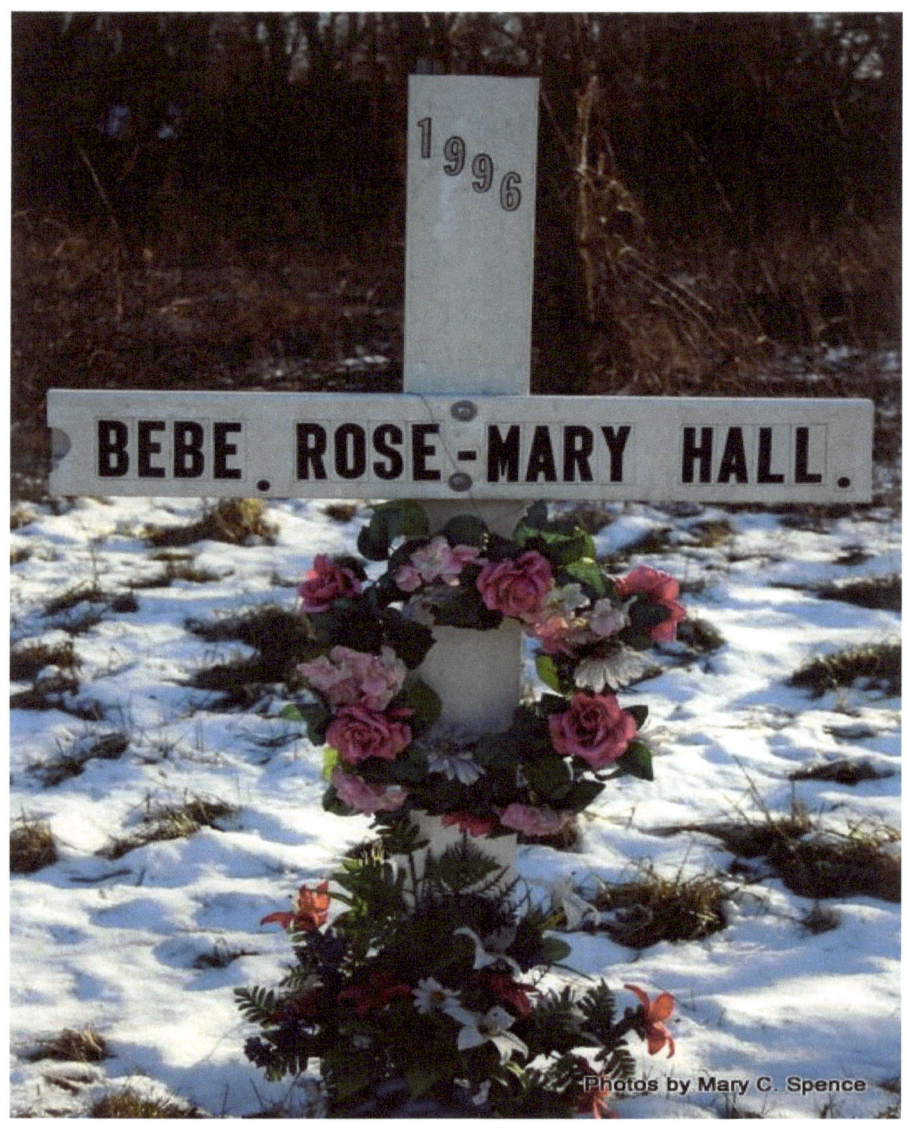

Photos by Mary C. Spence

ALONE

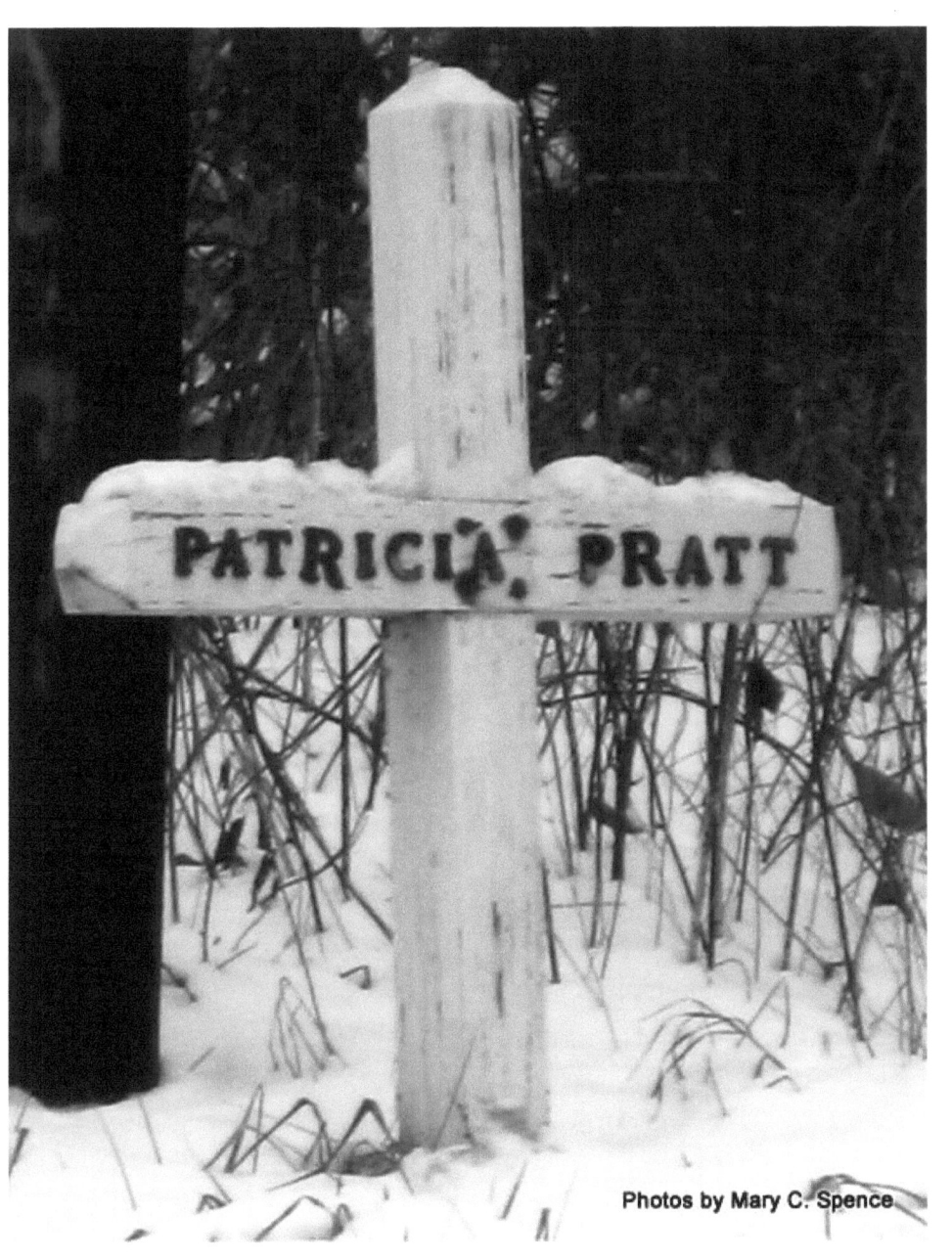

Photos by Mary C. Spence

Or long ago

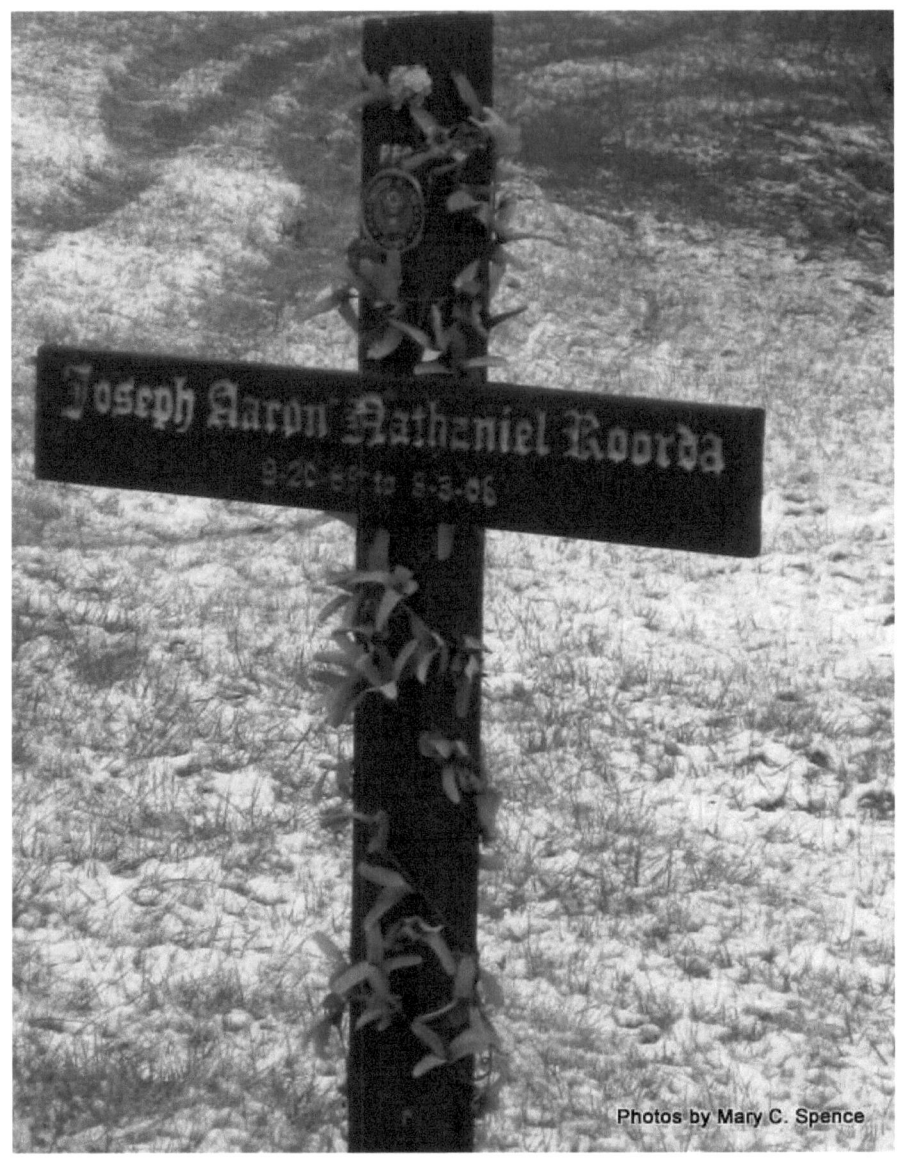

Joseph Aaron Nathaniel Roorda
9-20-89 to 8-3-06

Photos by Mary C. Spence

Male

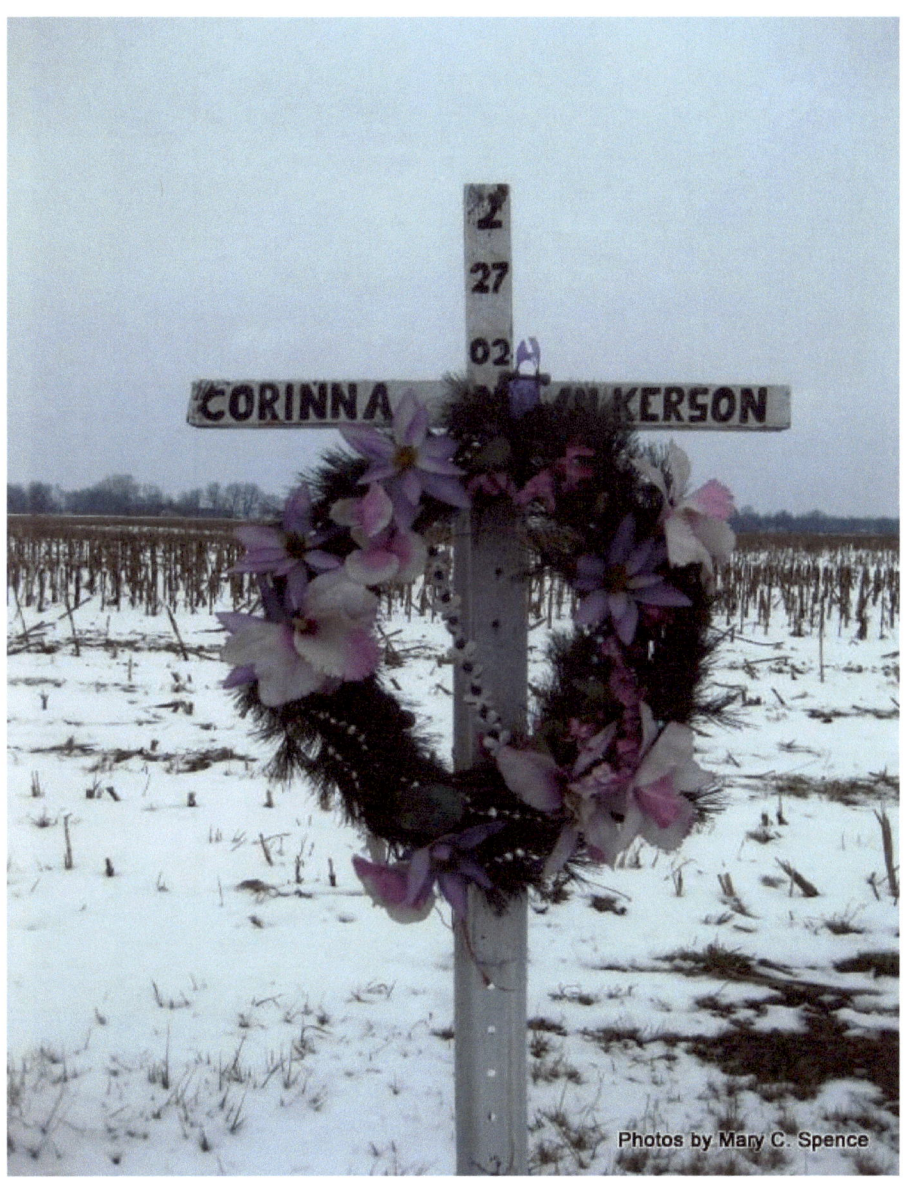

or Female

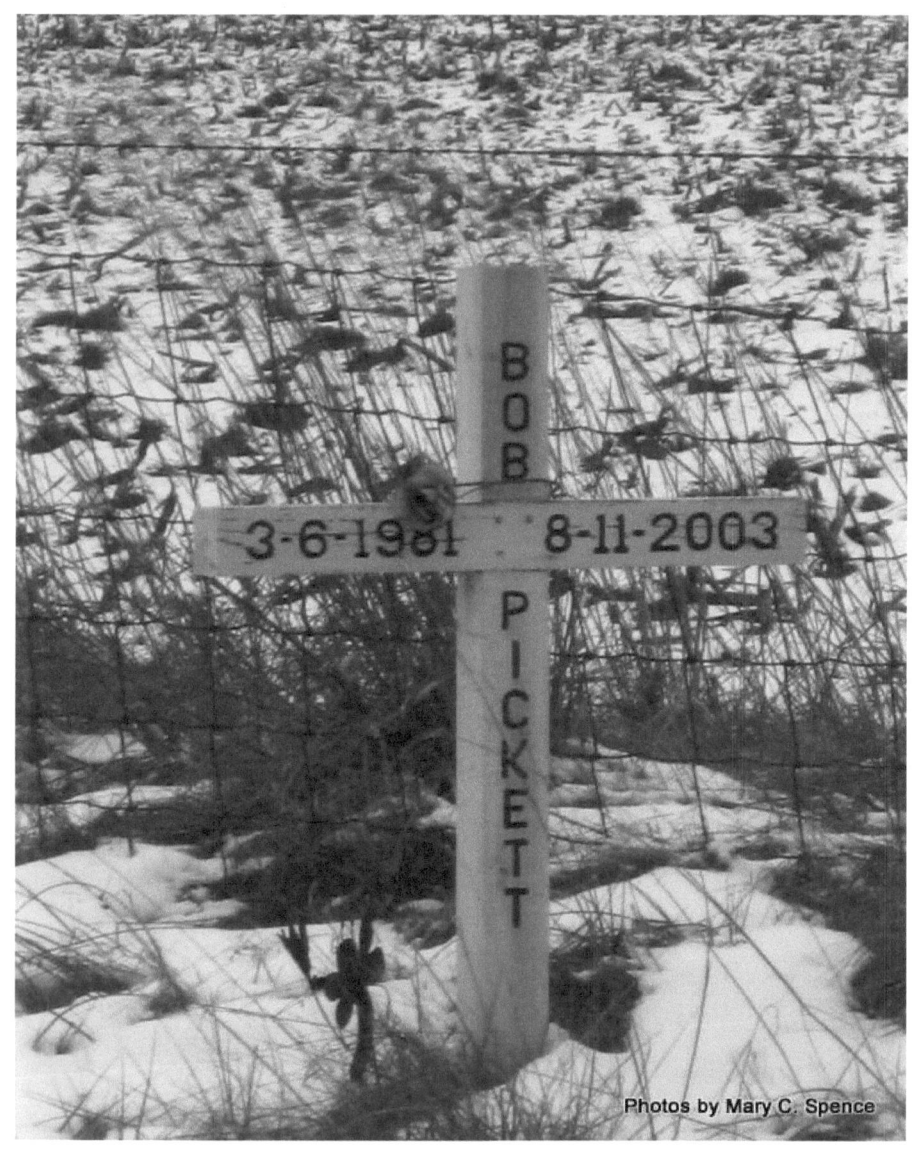

Photos by Mary C. Spence

Visible

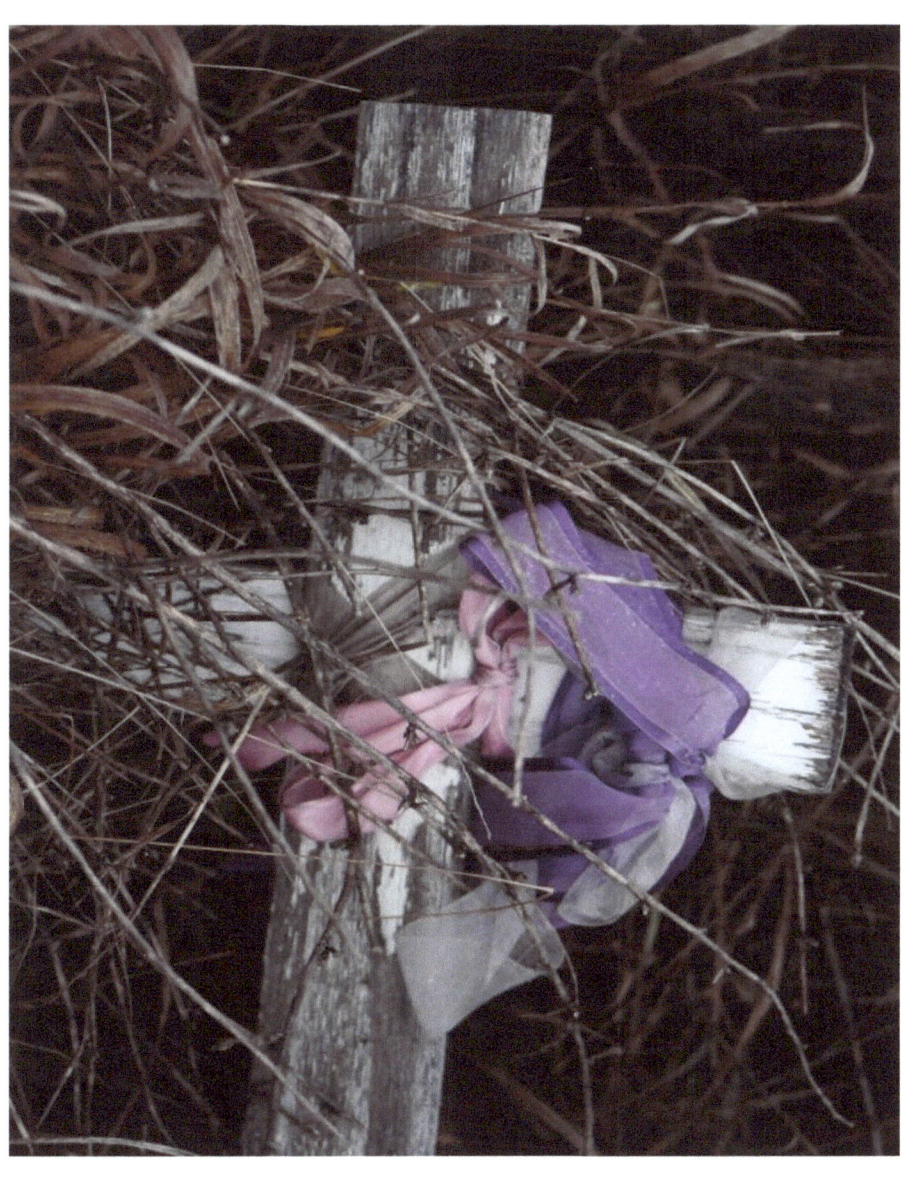

Or Hidden...
but not forgotten

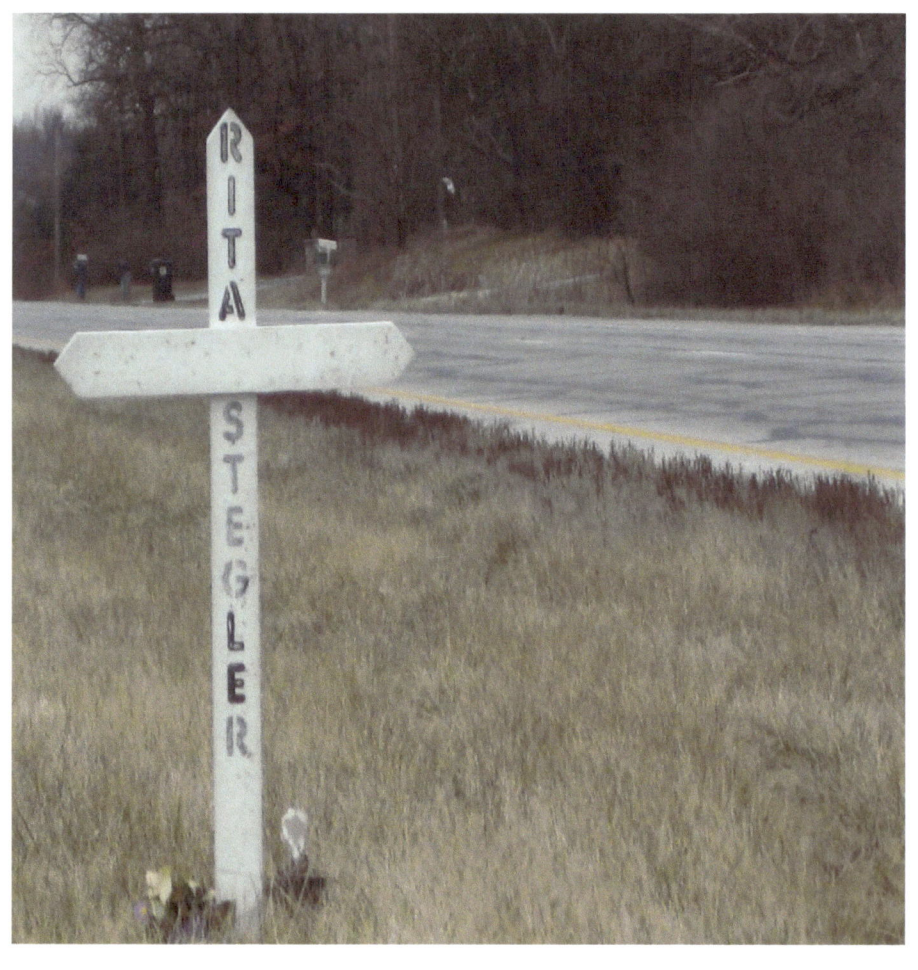

NO U-TURNS and
NO turning back the hands of time.

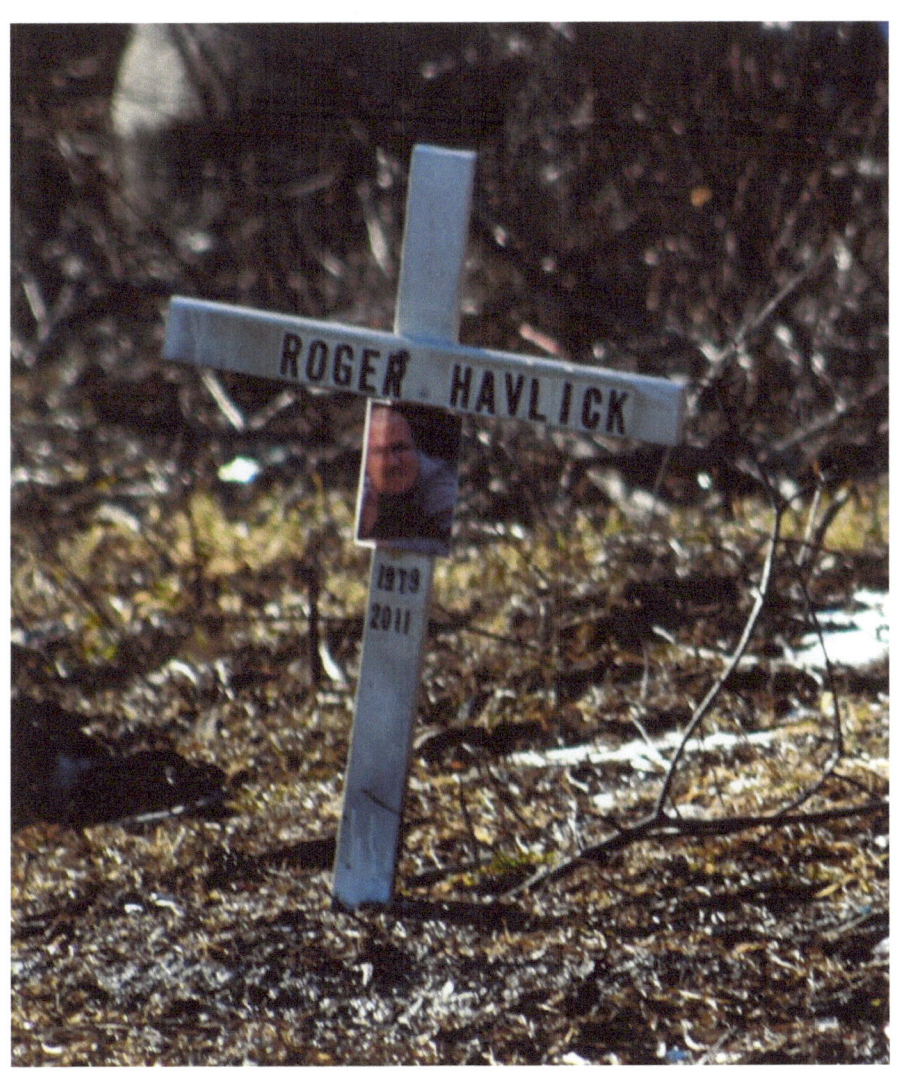

Round and round to sacred ground.

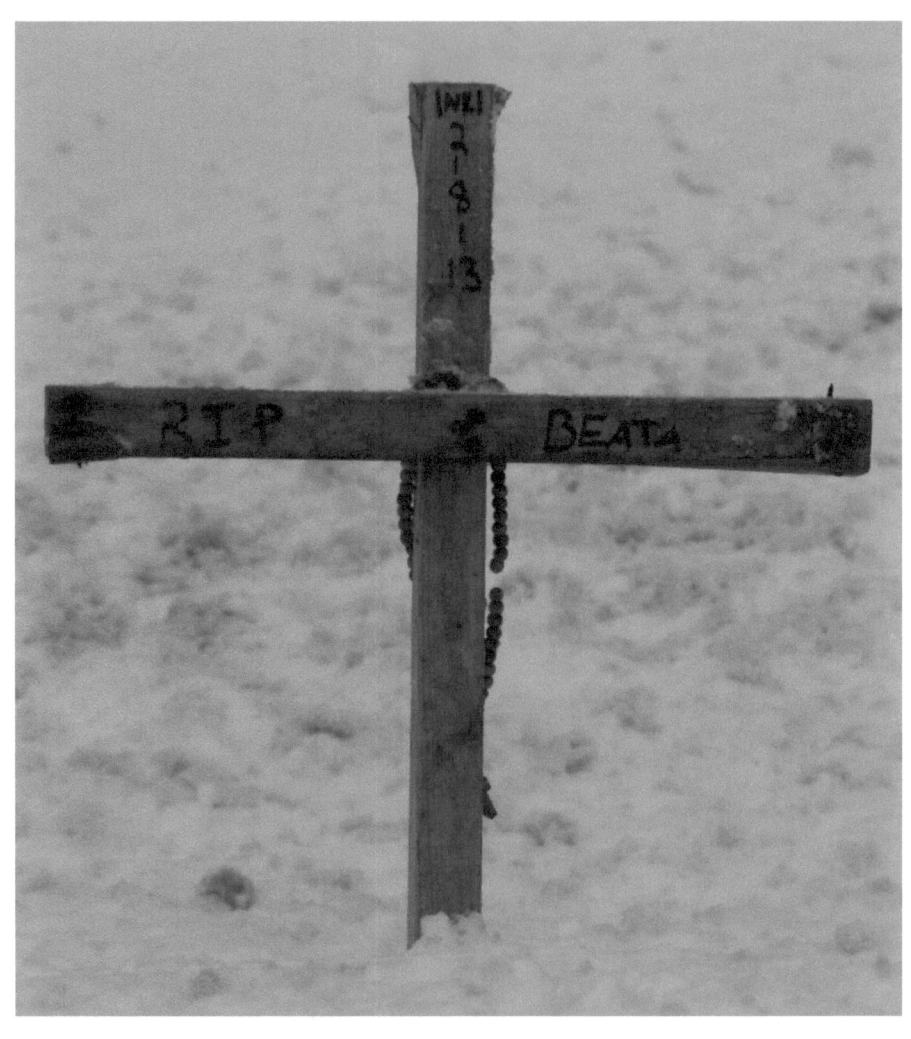

So sad and so close to home.

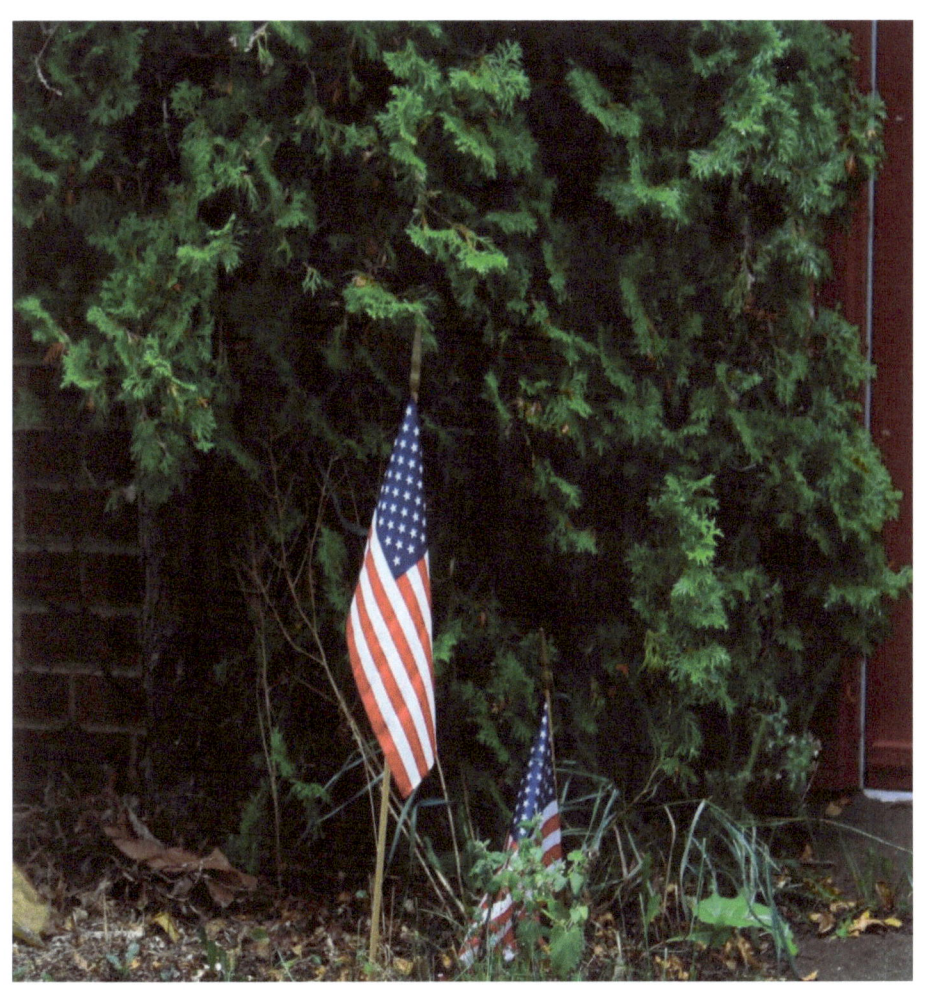

Marked by faith.

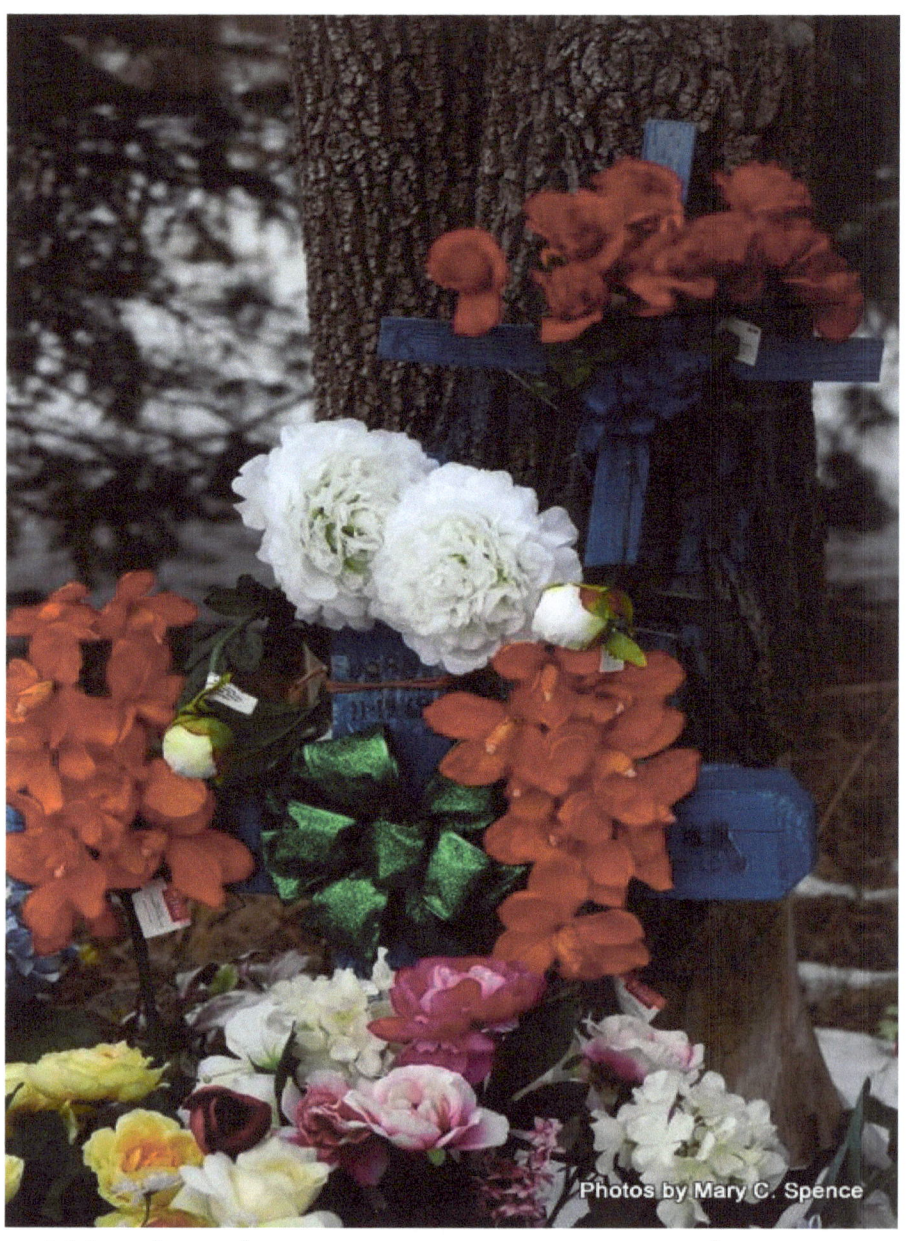

Photos by Mary C. Spence

We do what we can to remember everything.

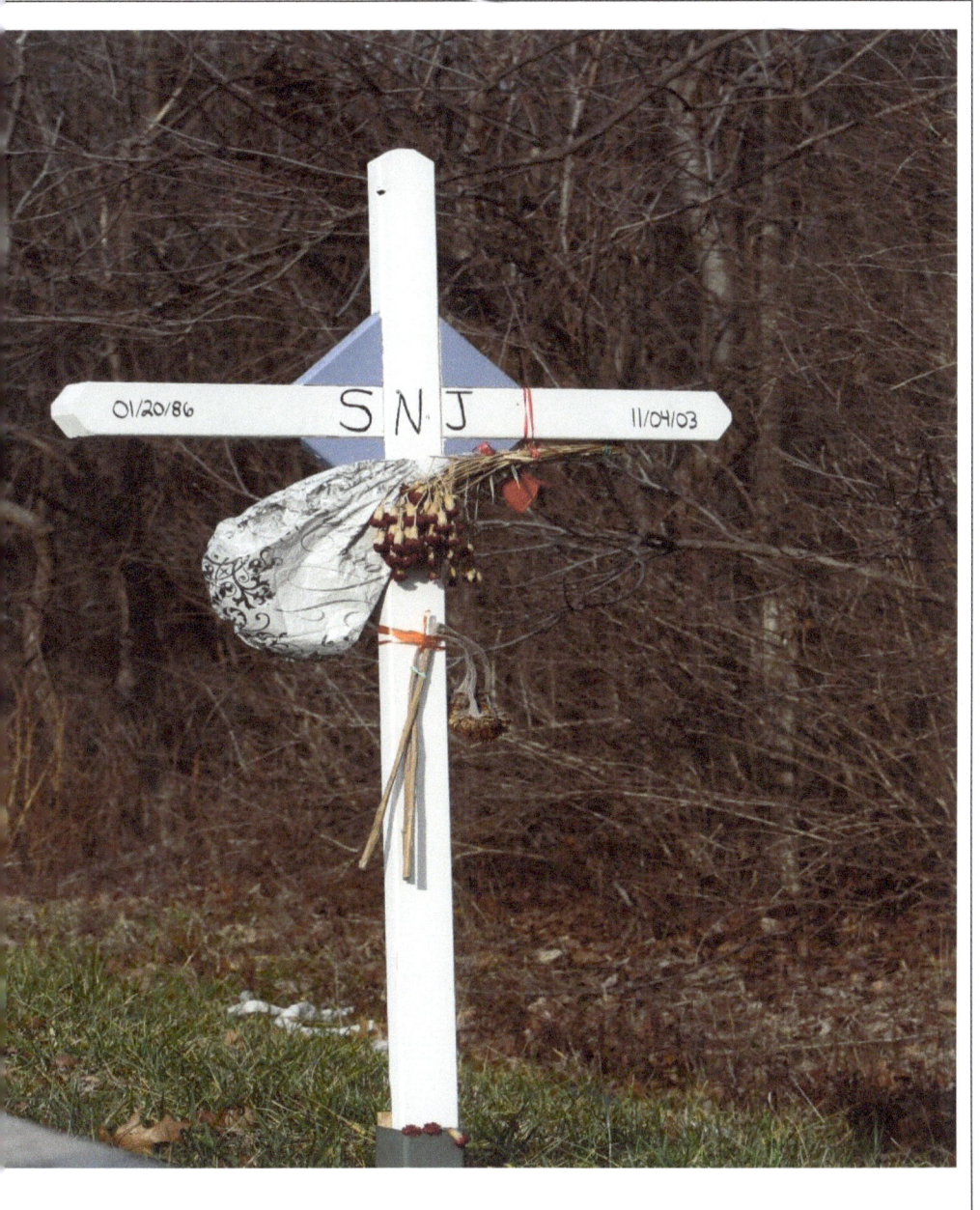

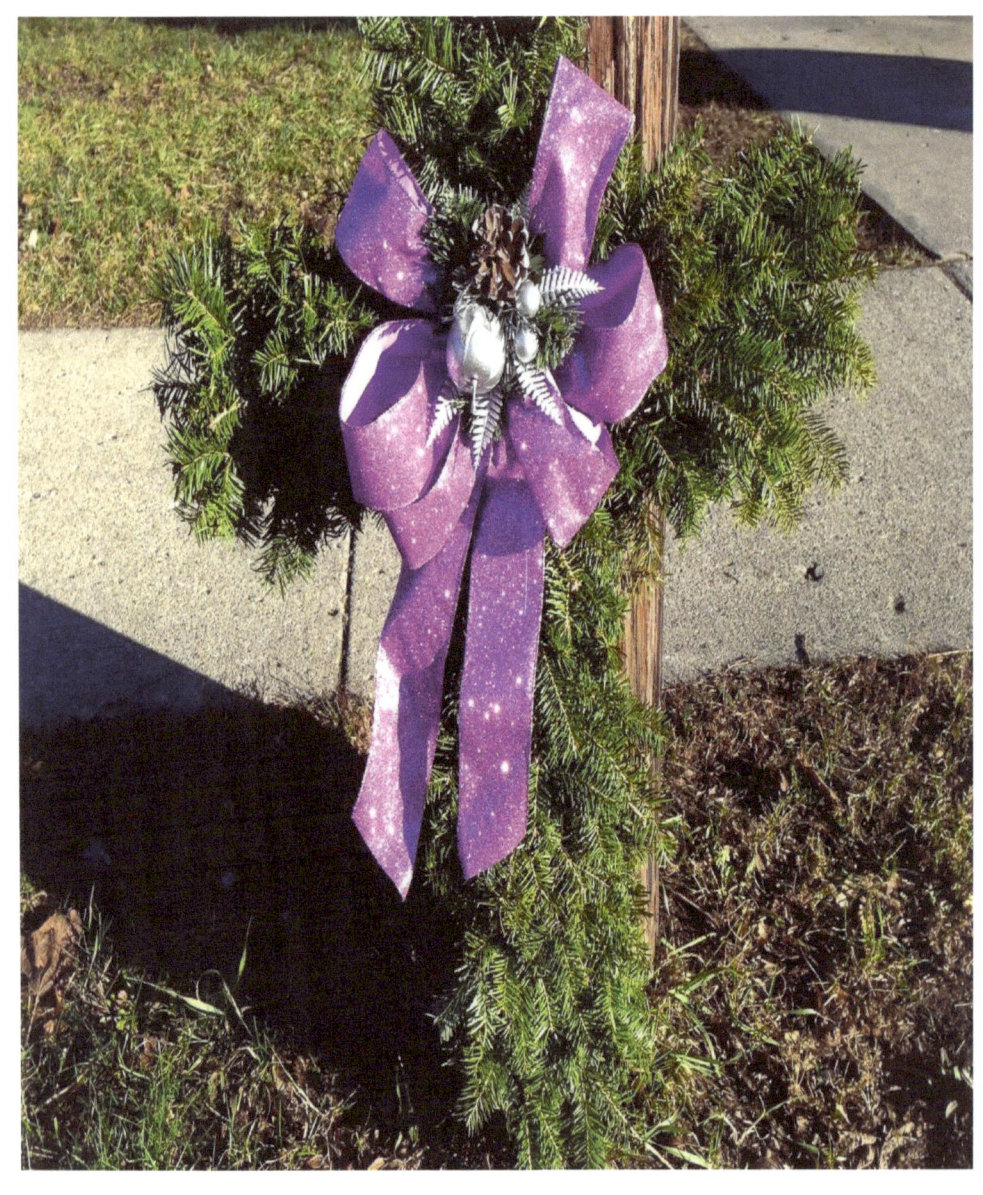

In every season

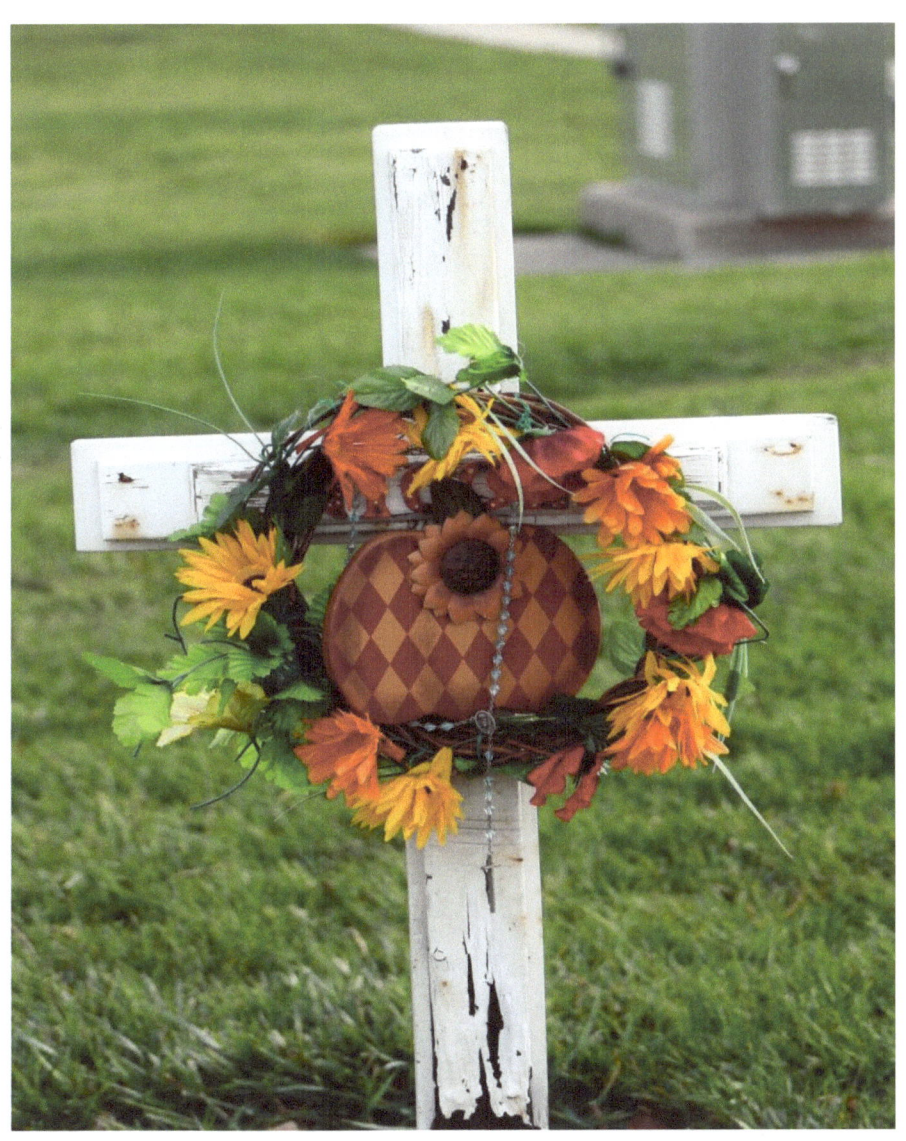

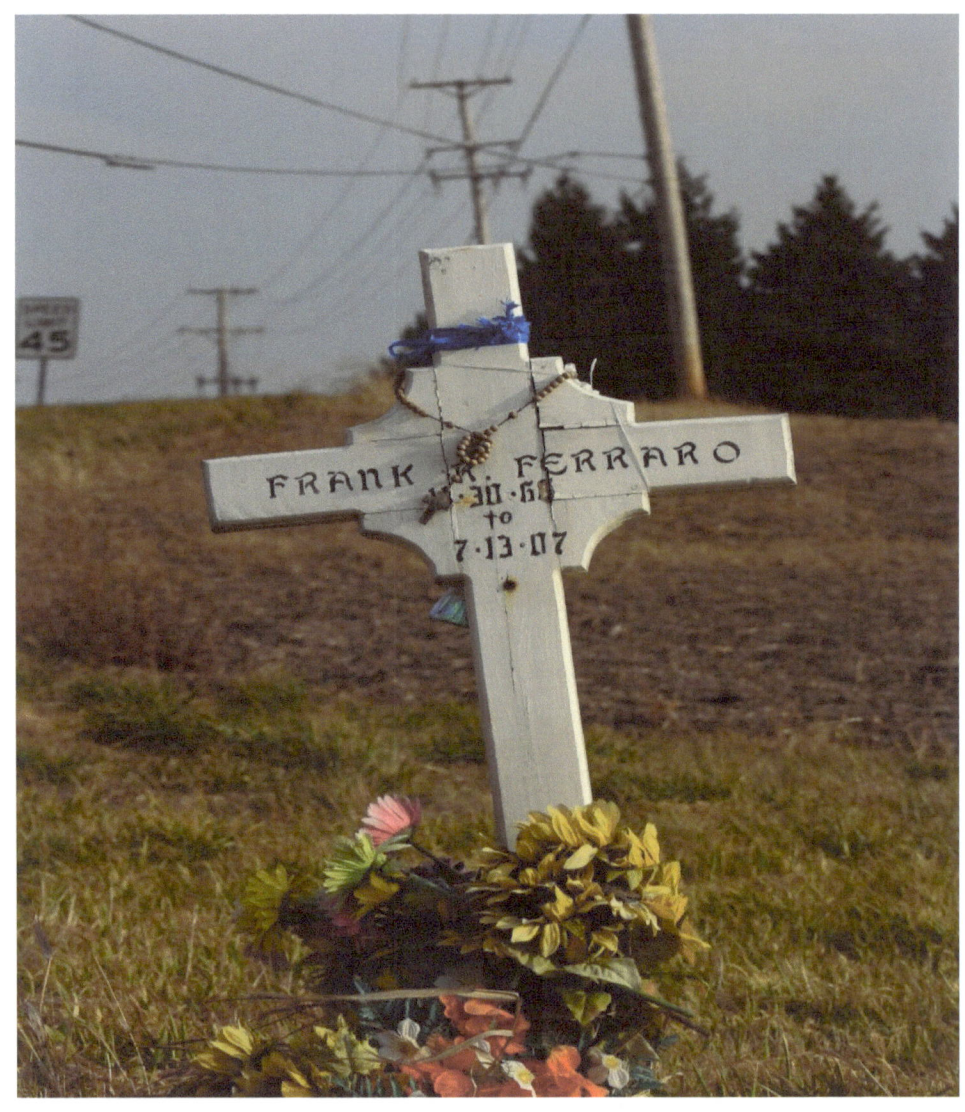

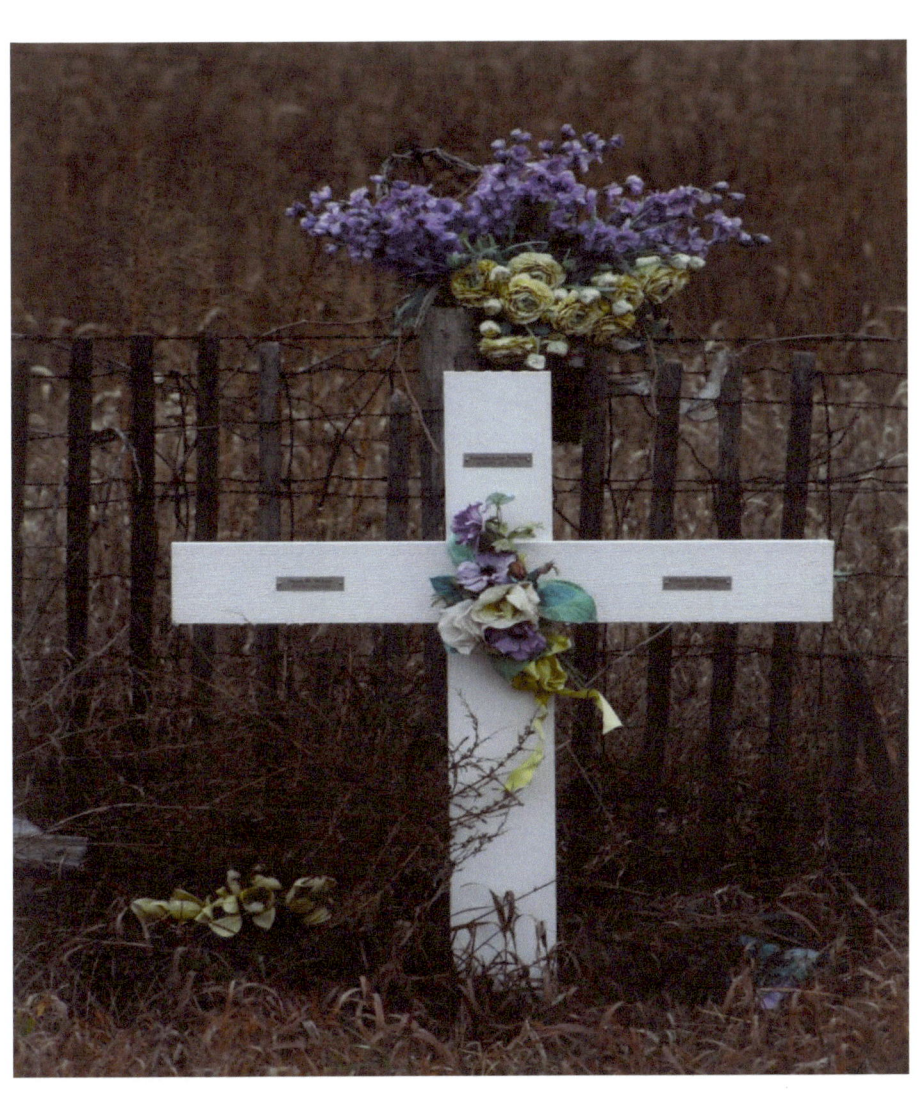

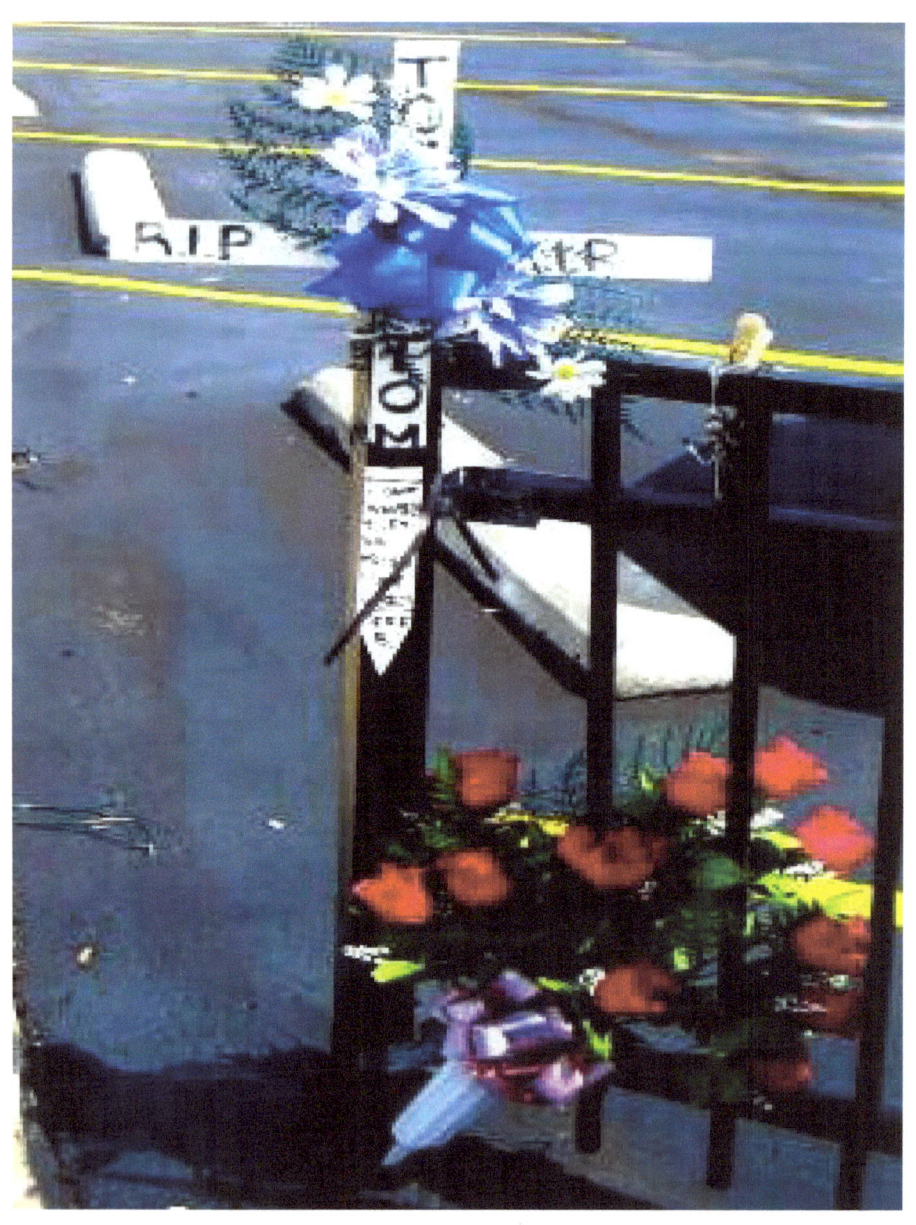

It's all that remains – L O V E

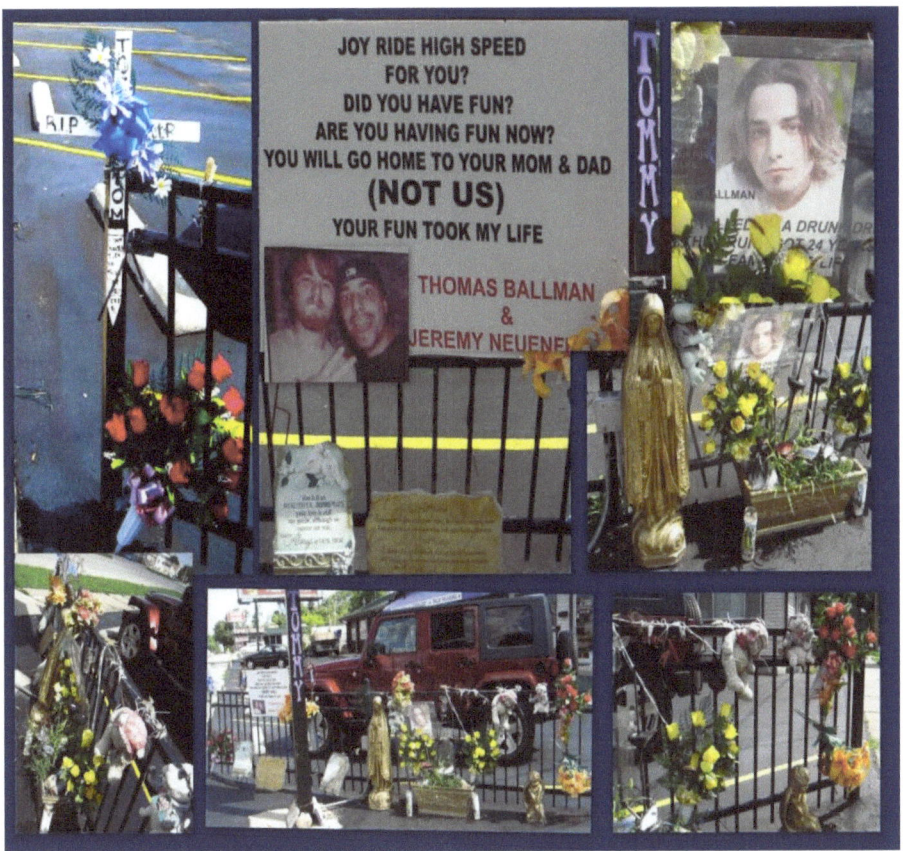

Seemed like there was a reason I got lost in Milwaukee...I couldn't believe my eyes when I happened upon this corner.

After reading the posted sign, I could feel their Mother's Sorrow... it's really sad and hard to imagine how much pain was left on the street...and in the hearts of their families, especially their Mothers.

Photographing crosses has become a journey.

www.AcrossAmerica-Home.com

Mary Spence's unique collection of colored photographs were taken with the help of her daughter Luanne, husband Michael, sister Anne and anyone else who was with her when she passed a cross, either turning the car around or driving slowly with camera in hand. Her variety of roadside crosses in this spiritual book reminds the readers as they turn each page that life is precious and transitory.

Since the name of the deceased person is written on each memorable cross, Mary's photography reaches out with compassion and sympathy to the grieving family members and friends. She subtly suggests with a thoughtful comment that the departed loved one has not been forgotten but exists in another dimension of reality with the Creator.

Nick Cibrario, author and artist